Two questions that set us free

Three inquires that lead the way

Paradigm shifts that open the door

"In our soul's evolutionary journey, each incarnation offers us the opportunity to broaden how we define ourselves." Dr. Steve Stroud's rich and thought-provoking book QUEST: Living an Enlightened Life in the Mundane World will take you on a journey of transformational discovery. Combining personal insight with scientific knowledge, he brings to life the human evolutionary experience. Stroud offers engaging questions and practices throughout, highlighting subjects such as the body-mind connection, belief systems, karma and how we create our own reality, Stroud's QUEST is a great companion to those wanting to deepen their experience towards living a more mindful and conscious life.

- Megan Skinner, author and Spiritual Counselor

STEVE STROUD ND, LAc

QUEST

LIVING AN
ENLIGHTENED
LIFE
IN THE MUNDANE WORLD

ISBN 978-1-7341128-0-1

Editing by David B. Scholsser
Book Design by Damonza

FIRST EDITION
Printed in the United States

www.stevestroud.org

CONTENTS

Part Five | 153

DEDICATION

To those people and events in my life where I have experienced kindness, truth, support, and forgiveness.

Especially to my daughter Crystal, Jahsun, and my grandkids Tejah and Ziven. To my wife Carrie - thank you for holding me in the comfort of your love. And to Annie, Karsten, Jonah, and Molly for allowing me to practice what I preach.

Thank you for inspiring me.

INTRODUCTION

This is more than a book for you to read. This is a journey to take. A great quest, if you will, into the very nature of your being and the known and unknown potential that resides within.

This is a guidebook on the practice and the journey of broadening awareness, honing mindfulness, and touching into the soulful and courageous endeavor of transforming our mundane life into an enlightened adventure.

This adventure before you will require faith and heartfelt effort. It will require a fair amount of practice, which is supported by the exercises sprinkled throughout the book. Some chapters offer contemplative exercises, others offer opportunities to practice the paradigm shifts the book presents.

The intention is to use these practices as guideposts to deepen your mindful engagement.

Consider this soulful journey akin to climbing a great mountain. There will be hills and deep caves, barren stretches and lush forests. It will be challenging as well as rewarding. By engaging in this journey, you will be afforded wider perspectives and inspiring views of yourself and the world around you.

In addition to holding this as a book, you will get the most from the experience of interacting with these words and ideas if you have a journal. If you don't already have a journal, reward and invest in yourself by finding a notebook and pen that feel good when you use them together.

FOREWORD

By Robert Anderson, M.D.

My family medical practice career, from which I am now retired, developed in a fairly routine and expected way until I attended a conference featuring biofeedback. I encountered a persuasive salesperson at that conference and returned home toting a biofeedback device. I paid it no heed for a couple of months before I found time to read the instruction manual. The directions told me to hold the finger thermometer with my right thumb and third finger for five minutes and write down my beginning skin temperature. Then I was to close my eyes and for 10 minutes silently repeat the phrases: "My hands are warm; my hands are warm; I am quiet, comfortable and relaxed; my hands are warm; I am quiet, comfortable and relaxed." However, by six minutes I became so bored that I prematurely opened my eyes. My skin temperature had risen 13 degrees Fahrenheit in those six minutes! My suspicions about the whole process melted away. As I became more adept at the process, I found that the same skin temperature rise occurred when I focused my consciousness on a meditative state.

After several weeks of continuing my meditative practice, I found I could reliably raise my temperature several degrees by simply evoking any quiet phrases in a quiet environment. Prior to this skin warming experience, my belief was that the dominant activity of the human nervous activity was unconscious, "automatic," and pre-determined. By contrast, my thermometer experience showed me that much of the nervous system activity must be consciously driven; and most of us haven't paid attention to the process which can be accessed in a meaningful way.

Some weeks later during my routine morning meditation, the diagnosis of a patient whose medical issues had me stumped spontaneously "popped" into my consciousness. From where it came, I could not fathom but it was very welcome. It felt like I was able to open a door into a whole new realm of consciousness. Some have described this as an "aha" experience. Other authorities have described this awareness as a state of mindfulness. Whatever the descriptor, it did feel to me like a voyage into a wider expansion of my experience.

This altered state has been called the "alpha" state of consciousness in which the basic brain rhythm slows in contrast to our usual "beta" state of consciousness.

Quest by Dr. Steve Stroud offers valuable practice and supportive suggestions so that readers can become adept students in finding that "zone" of alpha consciousness. With practice, as outlined in Quest, it becomes feasible for the expanded consciousness of the alpha state to predominate in contrast to the beta state of brain activity.

The implications of dropping into a rewarding balance of alpha and beta brain activity is worth every moment of attention in the quest to devote ourselves to living a life of enhanced enlightenment in what might be an otherwise mundane life experience.

Robert Anderson, M.D.

ROBERT ANDERSON, M.D. Past president of the American Holistic Medical Association and the founder of the American Board of Integrative Holistic Medicine. Books include *Clinician's Guide to Holistic Medicine (2001)* and *Stories of Healing, (2011)*.

PART ONE

The Great Quest

1

Quest

Everything you possess of skill, and wealth, and handicraft,
wasn't it first merely a thought and a quest?

—Rumi

IT WAS A rainy day, in a long procession of rainy days that morph and mist the passage of time, blurring Tuesday into Thursday without even a notice that, surely, there must have been a Wednesday in there somewhere.

Torrent sheets of wind-driven rain alternated with the ever-present fog, streaking the windows of perception, lulling my consciousness into the narcotic doldrums of day-to-day life.

So busy with the modern day task of survival — working at an auto parts store, trying to figure out how to be a dad, seeing if that cheap old Fiat would run another month — I was paying little attention to anything in my busy mind other than the pressing details of life. At night, I would listen to the rhythm of the rain, allowing my awareness to fade into slumber.

It was in that space between the conscious and the dream that I would often hear a distant conversation. Not quite a voice, not quite a sound. More like a message, telegraphed in some sporadic and seemingly random fashion, beckoning to me, tapping on the door, rattling like the rain against the transom of my consciousness.

It is the universe that calls to us; it is our soul that stirs in response.

It is a call intent on reminding us of the essence of who we are in this human incarnation. It is a call that reminds us that we are, at the core of our soul, enlivened beings. We are seekers; we are adventurers.

The calling is both unique and universal. It takes on as many distinct tones as there are individuals on this planet. At the same time, it produces a recognizable timbre that resonates in all souls.

It is a beckoning most often heard in those quiet spaces between our thoughts.

It is the call homeward.

We are cast into this physical form, like dust blown from the hand of God, into the soil of the material world to grow and experience life under the sun. Incarnated by choice, into this planet of duality, the life set before us is our soul's journey. From our first inspiration to our last exhalation, it is a voyage swelled by the winds of all that is possible and buffeted by the storms of that which is probable.

We are cast into this adventure not so much to discover the meaning of life, but to uncover, with awareness, those experiences which make our life meaningful. Not unlike spawning salmon, we navigate through life, mysteriously drawn by an innate homing device, beckoning our soul to return to its place of origin.

It is a journey that we have done before and know well but have no recollection of.

It is a journey that, if traversed with consciousness, will bring us many riches, though not necessarily material wealth.

The nature of the agreement we make prior to incarnating into the human form is to cast aside precognition of the life we have chosen. Thus, this journey into this unknown life affords us the freedom of choice, or free will, to experience that which is probable *and* to strive for that which is possible.

If this were not so, we would end up living our life marked only by the passage of time, as though our lives were akin to watching reruns on TV. Without this precognition of the incarnational experience, we learn as we go, picking up wisdom and experience — or, at least picking up experience.

We are called to get from here to there, often without a sense of where there is, and without knowing how to do what we are called to do.

We are often driven and commonly drawn, but surprisingly complacent as to the unfolding of our life's journey. Lulled by the narcotic effect of day-to-day life, it takes a persistent and compassionate universe, calling to us its siren song, calling for us to consciously partake in our journey home.

The universe is superbly patient. It has no demand that we respond to this calling today or tomorrow, in this life or the next. The universe seems unattached to the outcome of our lives. It seems more interested in the process of the journeys of our lives, and in providing transformational opportunities that offer us the adventure to insightfully navigate the mystical path home.

Standing in that damp and musty house, looking out into the dark night at the ever-present rain, a thought, like the passing mist, crossed my mind. Zen-kōan like — intriguing, though not particularly profound — echoing through the mists of eons, the thought was this:

"How long has it taken you to get to where you are?"

It was at that moment that I realized I had journeyed a millennial of lifetimes: a soul through the ages, gazing into a cold Northwest night, alone with my thoughts and the sounds in my head. What was that sound? Was it the resonance of the rain or the hum of the universe? Was there a difference?

Not really.

What mattered was that I was listening. I heard the calling, that whispering, enticing, beckoning, soul-stirring, enlivening call.

From both the personal and collective human consciousness point of view, we are entering a profound period of transformation. As is true of all transformational periods, this one has particular characteristics. The factors that flavor and distinguish each of our evolutionary periods can be seen in the alignment of the moon and the stars. It is reflected in a shift of individual awareness and in our current stage of human evolution. The words that best describe this current period's characteristics are: Quest and Great.

Or, more accurately: The Great Quest.

Somewhere in our individual and collective awareness is the sense, a calling, a longing for our lives to be engaged in some Great Quest.

Even if — in this precise moment — there is no sense of this in your life, take heed.

The time is ripe for such an adventure.

2

Awaken

And maybe it's the time of year, yes,
and maybe it's the time of man.

—Crosby, Stills, Nash and Young

TRANSFORMATIONAL WORK AND the quest to live mindfully demand that we broaden how we habitually define ourselves. One of the ways we identify ourselves is through the constellation of our thoughts, our feelings, and our actions. Through the process of incarnation our body — along with its personality — becomes the soul's manifestation into the physical world.

This manifestation is uniquely characterized by the expression of our thoughts, feelings, and actions. Here is a simple example of this idea in action.

The universe presents the exact same opportunity to two different people. Because they are different manifestations of thoughts, feelings, and actions, they respond differently:

1. "I think people from foreign countries are interesting, but because they are so different from me, I sometimes feel shy — even scared — and so I don't really interact with them."

2. "I think people from foreign countries are interesting, and I always feel excited to chat with them."

Presented with the same opportunity, each individual is uniquely defined by a constellation of thoughts, feelings, and actions.

Practice:

Find a contemplative spot and devote some time to writing responses to the following prompts in your journal. Use the framework of your thoughts, feelings, and actions.

1. Describe yourself in a short paragraph.

2. Describe yourself in a sentence.

3. Describe yourself in one word.

An Incarnational Opportunity

In our soul's evolutionary journey, each incarnation offers us the opportunity to broaden how we define ourselves. To do so, the universe offers us the chance to bring forth un-evolved aspects of ourselves. These undeveloped aspects commonly manifest in any of these three ways:

1. Limiting thought patterns.

2. Unresolved feelings (what many people call "emotional baggage").

3. Repetitive actions that sabotage our best intentions.

Imagine the soul arriving into each incarnation with suitcase in hand. In that suitcase are any number of thoughts, feelings, and actions waiting to be unpacked.

They are ready for the opportunity to evolve.

Each soul's case is packed with thoughts, feelings, and actions that in previous lives created pain or separation, or just did not develop. These un-evolved thoughts, feelings, and actions will — in this life — continue to cause pain and separation until enough faith, energy, insight, and grace create the synchronicity for their development and transformation.

In this life, we can unpack and use the manifest world as a tool to develop these emerging aspects and thus broaden how we define ourselves. These yet-to-manifest aspects, sleeping in the basement of our subconscious, are the harbinger of our evolutionary journey. They are held with honor and in trust by our soul. They journey with us from life to life.

Our life experiences in this physical world supply us with the opportunity to awaken into our consciousness a thought, a feeling, or an action that longs to evolve beyond the habit of pain and separation into the grace of healing and connection.

Question

Quaere is the root, from Latin, of the words question and query: to ask or seek. To further our Great Quest, the valuable query would be:

> *What undeveloped thought, feeling, or action —*
> *should it awaken into my consciousness — will*
> *broaden my life in a consequential way?*

A thought evokes a feeling, which inspires an action.

Thoughts

Our thoughts create the construct of our reality. Thoughts provide us with a model of the world we experience and an interpretation of it.

In discovering our Great Quest, we ask:

What thought — should it awaken into my consciousness — will broaden my life in a consequential way?

This thought may come to us in several ways. It is that inner voice of guidance, that small voice we hear in moments of contemplation. It is the voice that plants the seeds of ideas. It is the voice that whispers directions. It might be a familiar voice, perhaps one you have known since childhood. It might be a new thought, freshly unpacked and placed into the cognitive aspect of your mind.

It was late that cool and clear autumn night. I scuffed my way through the piles of fallen leaves, walking home from a loud fraternity party. I craved some quiet. I sprawled across the damp grass under an inky splash of shadow. Others came and went in boisterous groups. Infatuated lovers strolled by hand in hand. An occasional student walked briskly, head down, earnestly toting his books.

These distractions began to fade as I opened my senses to the dark night and the stars above.

"OK," I said. "I'm ready," I spoke to no one, yet hoped someone, something would hear me.

I lay there listening, straining to receive a message, a voice, a calling, a direction. Some seed of an idea that would connect me to some great cosmic awareness.

"What is my place here in this life?"

I'm ready.

"What is my place…."

I had the thought that, should I petition the universe, I would receive my answers. I had expected — perhaps naively — that the universe would hold a flashing sign: "This is the way. Here are the steps you must take to live happily ever after. Here is the reason you are alive."

I petitioned the universe for The Answer, imagining it would come to me in a light-bulb moment.

Startled awake a short time later, I was cold and stiff. I found my way back to the dorm. I woke hours later, still fully dressed. Unaware that something consequential occurred that night, I returned to the mundane life of a freshman at college.

By all appearances, my petitioning of the universe had failed. I did not get any lightning bolt insights. I only realized that my evolutionary task did not lie in finding The Answer, but in being curious enough to ask the question.

How easily we dismiss insight when it does not arrive as we expect.

I "only" realized my evolutionary task….

That is a pretty valuable insight.

I "only" realized my evolutionary task…

…was to be curious enough to ask the question.

I realized that it is not answers that open our consciousness and deepen our insight. It is questions that spark the flame of enlightenment.

Yet there was more.

Had I stopped there; I would have missed the bigger harbinger of my evolutionary journey.

I would have caught the small fish and let the bigger fish get away. The big fish — the big transformational nugget, the life-changing mindful moment — is always evident, always obvious, and always simple. And because it is always evident, always obvious, and always simple, we frequently dismiss it.

When we start with the false premise that transformation is complicated, we derive a false conclusion. We convince ourselves that transformation is elusive, complex, takes struggle, and happens only to other — more fortunate and gifted — people.

Transformation might be challenging, but it is not complicated.

That, in its anti-climactic mundane presentation, was the thought that awakened into my consciousness and that profoundly broadened my life in a consequential way:

Transformation might be challenging, but it is not complicated.

And the other thought that awakened into my consciousness:

Questions — not answers — are the key to opening our perception.

The universe patiently and consistently offers moments for wisdom and transformation. Some moments are large. Some are small.

The Great Quest is to listen and respond to the inner voice that whispers directions.

So you can awaken into your consciousness.

A thought — large or small — can significantly affect your life in a consequential way.

The universe's calling — that inner guidance — created the thought that I should lie in an inky shadow on damp grass and petition the universe. I had wanted The Answer.

Instead, the universe whispered directions.

Where have you listened? And where have you turned a deaf ear? Have you dismissed that sweet inner voice? When the universe whispers its siren song, do you allow your soul to respond? Is there a thought or idea, a message or signal, a voice calling to you?

Will you allow yourself to listen?

Feelings

We make decisions based on how we believe a particular choice will make us feel. Car companies don't tell us the bore, stroke, and timing sequence of the engine. Instead, car companies tell us how happy, powerful, or independent we will feel when we own that car. In deciding the nature of our Great Quest, we ask:

> *What feeling — should it awaken into my consciousness — will broaden my life in a consequential way?*

Her hair was coffee brown. Her skin was fair. She smiled as though she knew the answer to some great mystery and was bemused that no one else had riddled it out.

We sat next to each other in science class with Mr. Kidwell, who had a penchant for odd things like opening the blinds when it started to snow and growing purple potatoes. We sat together in algebra, where the ancient and chalk-covered Mrs. Nockman scratched hieroglyphic formulas on the blackboard. We loosely hung in the same circles as we wandered the halls between classes.

I was in eighth grade and had a major crush going.

I watched my friends and classmates fall in and out of crushes. In pairs and in groups, they laughed and tousled and touched with an ease of expression that I could not grasp. I could sense my desire to feel such flow yet seemed incapable of bringing such feeling into manifestation. I felt love. I was a 14-year-old boy and crazy in love.

For some, feeling love may be their Great Quest. For me, it's about expressing love, not about feeling love. The yet-to-manifest *feeling* that wandered the hallways of my heart, striving for release, was the simple desire to express how I felt.

Participating in life's Great Quests will yield great accomplishments. The universe, though, in its wisdom, is less attached to what we accomplish and more interested in how we get from Point A to Point B. The universe, supporting our soul's evolution, offers us opportunities to develop aspects of ourselves that will significantly broaden our life in a consequential way.

Today, I express my love more easily than I did yesterday. Tomorrow, my quest is to express it even more organically. And I know that the universe will challenge me to up my game.

There is no evolutionary growth for me in the department of expressing my love when things in my life and relationships are going well. I have noticed that the universe finds successively challenging opportunities for me to express how I feel. For it is when I experience conflicts, misunderstandings, and mischaracterizations that my angels pause to take note…. In the most challenging of times, am I able to arise to the challenge and express my love?

That is my Great Quest.

Is there a feeling waiting to manifest, wandering the hallways of your heart, striving for release? And in so doing, does it broaden how you define yourself? Is it to forgive when the impulse is to hate? Is it to feel patient when exasperated? Is it to love in the face of rejection?

Action

A thought evokes a feeling, which inspires an action. Manifestation into the physical world occurs through our actions. The physical world thus becomes the mirror and our learning lab, reflecting to us the effect of our archetypal thoughts, feelings, and actions.

What action — should it awaken into my consciousness
— will broaden my life in a consequential way?

There are many un-manifest thoughts, feelings, and actions archetypes that have tugged at the sleeve of our consciousness our entire life. They are as familiar now as when we were children. They thread their way from the playgrounds and study halls of our youth through our work, families, and friends of adulthood. They accompany us into elderhood.

Other thoughts, feelings, and actions come into our awareness at opportune times in our life. They arrive and board our consciousness like commuters on the Long Island Railroad, crowding for space, jostling for position hoping to break through the hypnotic hiss and rumble of our mundane life. Hoping to move to the front of our awareness, reach for the stop request cord, and debark at the crossroads of intention and heart.

It is only through faith and effort that we are able to manifest our thoughts and feelings.

What have you been itching to do? What adventure, mark, or desired impact rumbles through your inner world, searching for a venue to manifest?

Practice:

Listen to your inner voice.

Find a quiet spot indoors or in nature. Have a paper and pen, or an electronic tablet like an iPad or a smartphone.

Take a few moments to breathe deeply and relax your body. Take a breath and another and begin to listen. Allow the sounds inside your head and the sounds around you to fade together. Relax your throat and your shoulders. With pen and paper at the ready, allow yourself to free flow in thought, and — without editing — begin to write what you hear from the signal or voice that is currently calling you.

This voice may be new to your awareness or a familiar calling you have known your entire life:

Be great.

Be free.

Grow flowers.

Paint.

You are not alone.

You can do it.

Go to school.

Start your own business.

Listen to the universe.

Write that book.

Dance.

Help kids learn to read.

Love.

These thoughts are of divine calling. They become the threads that weave the tapestry of our experiences. Life will unfold whether we mindfully engage or not. To engage in weaving the great tapestry of your thoughts, you must listen.

Connect to your inner most feelings.

Find a quiet spot indoors or in nature. Have a paper and pen, or an electronic tablet like an iPad or a smartphone.

Take a meditative breath, and another, and center on the core of your body. With each breath, bring your awareness to the emotional/feeling aspect of your being. Begin to connect to the yet-to-manifest feeling deep within your emotional being that your soul has so sweetly carried from life to life.

Allow yourself these feelings. You have every right to have your feelings. They may cause a physical sensation in your body. Just witness it without judgment.

When ready, write — without editing — the feelings you would like to express but have yet to do so:

I love you.

I forgive you.

I am sorry.

Please forgive me

No!

I hate you.

I am sad.

I'm scared.

I am happy.

I am frustrated.

Your goal is authenticity. Being real is essential to being whole. You will not go to hell or be damned by the universe if you feel hate, frustration, or fear.

These are normal human emotions, though they may be inconvenient or physically uncomfortable. Feeling an emotion such as hate is very different than being hateful.

Once I realized I could own the feeling of hate — even if it was towards someone I cared about— it cracked open my ability to feel a wide variety of emotions. These feelings are the pigments that enrich the colors of our experiences. These are hues that tint the tapestry of our life. I understood that, to the degree I suppressed my uncomfortable feelings — hate, anger, frustration — I suppressed to the same degree my pleasurable feelings — love, joy, enthusiasm.

At that point, I began to allow myself to feel what I authentically felt.

Authenticity is exceptionally liberating. And it allowed me to authentically love.

From the feelings you have written, practice expressing them through voice or demonstration. Start small. Maybe you are your first audience. Or go big and shout them from the top of the mountain.

Manifestation

Here, action is required.

Life is an interactive endeavor. It's a contact sport.

The final piece of embarking on any Great Quest is taking that first physical step — often, the most challenging. Stifled by fear, distracted by what others think, we may confess that we don't know what to do.

Here, a challenge arises.

It is rare, in a mindful life, that we don't know what to do.

It is common, however, that we are afraid to do it.

Acknowledge the fear. Allow yourself to know. Breathe.

The difference between fear and excitement is that with fear we hold our breath. With excitement, even though we experience the same physical sensations, we are able to breathe.

Listen to that inner voice, feel that unfamiliar feeling. Create your life. Make that call, grab that shovel. Walk through the door and ask for what you want. Leave a stifling relationship. Get married. Sit in that chair and write that book.

In your journal, write these prompts and your responses:

This is the action that I am currently taking:

This is the action I will manifest this week:

This is the action I will manifest this month:

This is the action I will manifest this year:

A Worthy Adventure

Whatever it is — whatever un-manifest thought, feeling, or action beckons to you — whatever it is that stirs your soul — never lose sight that we are indeed seekers and adventurers at the core of our being.

We are cast into the world of manifestation to navigate the currents of experience and opportunity, seeking the slipstream of awareness, moving homeward towards the sea of enlightenment. It takes a place of stillness, between the awake and the dream, to hear the call. This Great Quest takes great dedication, due diligence, clear intention, unwavering faith, and an open heart.

By intentionally engaging in our Great Quest, we awaken from our slumber and begin to respond to that universal calling.

We begin to recognize the path that will take us on our journey home, and we begin to recognize the riches along the way.

Our life journey becomes a worthy adventure.

Our Great Quest becomes a quest to connect with the greatness within us simply because we have chosen, with awareness, to become a significant and consequential force in our own life and — in doing so — we become a significant and consequential force in the lives of others.

The universe — that patient, undemanding, unattached universe — now beckons.

How will you journey the path that takes you home?

3

The Body-Mind Connection

*Your mind, emotions and body are instruments and the way
you align and tune them determines how well you play life.*

—Harbhajan Singh Yogi

OUR REPETITIVE BEHAVIORS reinforce specific neural pathways in
our brain. These neural pathways are bundles of fibers that transmit
messages. The more the neural synapses fire repeatedly in the same
stimulus-reaction pattern, the bigger the pathway becomes. Like
on-ramps of merging traffic, we funnel our behavior along the
most used path. These soon become the familiar highways of our
comfortable, locked-in habits. We become fixed in our thoughts
and fixed in our ways.

This stiffening of our view of reality is reflected in the stiffening
of our physical bodies.

Challenging this habitual tendency to crystallize into the physical body our thoughts, feelings, and actions is part of our quest to live a mindful life. Though there is much truth to the saying "you can't teach an old dog new tricks," the universe is ever patient in offering us opportunities to adapt and grow.

The more willing I am to exit the highway of habit and wander an unknown road, the more expansive my life becomes.

The more willing I am to open and challenge my belief systems, the more flexible my physical body becomes.

Any living organism, when faced with adverse or demanding circumstances, either will adapt to those circumstances or die. Life is an interactive sport. The dynamic nature of it offers us a steady diet of opportunities to evolve and expand how we define ourselves and how we relate to the world around us. Our awareness and understanding of reality are — we are hopeful — ongoing, evolving, dynamic processes. Were this not true, we would not adapt and grow but stiffen, wither, stagnate, and die.

Adapt or Die

The large windows of the old school building overlooked a tree-covered ravine and the urban hills of north Seattle. A few autumn leaves of yellow and brown clung stubbornly to the branches, though their fate was not in question. The changing seasons — a demanding situation in its own right — meant that these lingering leaves would soon join their kin on the nearby sidewalks and lawns.

I had just finished my first quarter in naturopathic medical school. Eleven more quarters to go.

As I watched the dance of the falling leaves, I contemplated the words of my biology professor. "Adapt or die," she had said in the first week of our training. Was she talking about biological cellular systems, or was she talking about us as first year medical students embarking on a Great Quest?

It is one and the same, I concluded.

Adapt or die became our class motto. It also became a guiding principle and a touchstone for living my life from a transformational point of view. It is a foundational principle for living a mindful life.

For me to adapt, I knew I would have to exit the highway of habit. I would have to allow my reality to be flexible and to expand. What I knew, how I felt, what I did, who I was — for me to expand, I would have to challenge my reality. To challenge my reality, I would have to challenge my belief systems. A part of me knew, but had yet to fully grasp, I was entering the journey of personal transformation.

The Development of our Cellular Reactions, also known as our Belief Systems

In the development of our belief systems, it is from conception through the age of seven that we are most receptive to the influences from our environment. Our developing brain-wave patterns, neuronal expansion, and maturing human energy field (HEF, or aura) all support the fact that our early childhood years are the most impressionable of our entire life. By the age of seven, the constellations of our belief systems begin to solidify and lock into place.

Brain-wave Patterns

The human brain has four main brain-wave patterns. These wave patterns correlate to levels of conscious activity. These waves are described by *amplitude* (how big) and *frequency* (how often). There are big waves that rise and fall slowly. These have high amplitude and low frequency. Small waves that occur in rapid succession have low amplitude and high frequency. The high-amplitude/low-frequency Delta wave pattern resembles the movement of a large ocean swell. Slowly rising high above the horizon and slowly falling deep beneath the horizon. It is like the slow plucking of a bass guitar or the resonance of a bass drum. Towards the other end of the brain-wave scale is the low amplitude, high frequency wave pattern found in Alpha. This pattern has numerous small waves that occur in rapid succession. It is like a buzzing bee, a quick guitar lick or the crescendo of a snare drum.

Visually, the four kinds of brain waves appear like this:

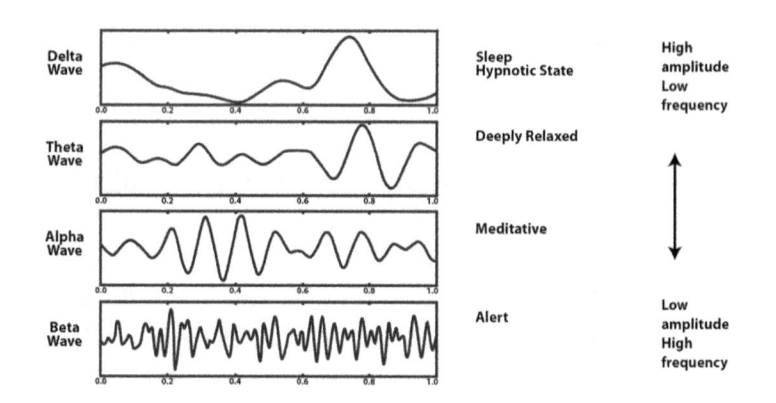

Different brain-wave patterns dominate during different stages of human development, as the following chart shows.

Age in Years	Brain Wave	Cycles per Second	Level of Brain Activity		Number of Repetitions Required to Adopt New Behaviors
0 to 4	Delta	0.5 to 5	Deep sleep. Subjective non-physical states of existence.		Not applicable
4 to 7	Theta	4 to 7	Dreams, hypnotic. Reality created through imagery.		1 to 2
8 to 14	Alpha	7 to 14	Relaxed, alert. Receptive and absorbent mental state.		About 21
15+	Beta	14 to 21	Normal awake. Left-brain conscious mind.		Thousands

Nervous system A review of the universe - Urban Child Institute

Delta brain wave (deep sleep): 0.2-3.0 hertz

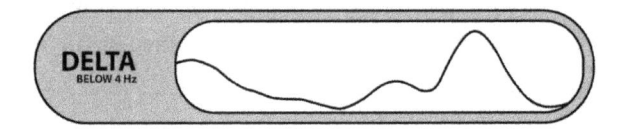

These waves are like the ocean swell, long and slow. Delta waves are often associated with being fast asleep, hyper-relaxed, or in a deep meditation. Delta waves are the dominant brain wave in babies.

Theta brain wave (dreaming): 3.0-8.0 hertz

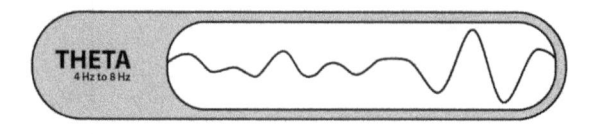

Theta waves indicate a normal or light sleep, drowsiness or daydreaming, and creative and imaginative thinking that is led by the subconscious (for example, the "eureka moment," when ideas suddenly come to us). This suggests that Theta waves allow for easier communication between the conscious and subconscious minds. This is the standard frequency range for children between the ages of four and seven years.

Alpha brain wave (relaxed): 8.0-12.0 hertz

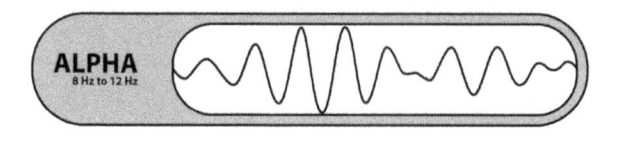

In Alpha waves, we begin to see more frequent, smaller waves. They are associated with a fully awake and conscious but relaxed state of mind. When you get back from school or work, when you sit and share your day with family or friends, your brain waves will be in the Alpha range. This is the typical relaxation range for anyone older than about 13.

Beta brain wave (awake and alert): 12.0-38.0 hertz

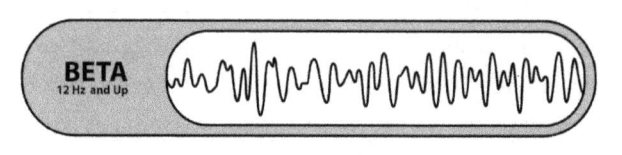

Beta waves have high frequency and low amplitude (or size). They are characteristic of an engaged mind that is alert and well-focused. These are the dominant waves most of us will experience during the day. They are produced when our attention is directed to the outside world. They are also used in complex problem-solving, having conversations, any form of active exercise (using motor skills), and in learning new information and skills. Towards the upper end of its range, Beta brain waves can indicate stressed or anxious thoughts.

The brain-wave physiology of our stimulus-reaction pattern

As we look at challenging our habitual stimulus-reaction patterns, it's critical to note the correlation between brain-wave frequencies and the number of repetitions required for new behavior.

"Number of repetitions" denotes how often a person's brain must perceive, or be introduced to, a specific stimulus to create a specific behavior. The number of repetitions needed to create or change behavior is significantly less in the Delta and Theta frequencies. Delta brain waves make up the predominant frequencies in the first four years of life. Influences and information are absorbed much more quickly in these lower frequency brain-wave patterns then in the higher frequency Alpha and Beta waves that are more predominant in adulthood.

From age four to seven, children operate for the most part in the Theta range. Their brain waves run between four and seven cycles per second. These are large, slow waves. In this state, humans need only one or two experiences of learning to create or change a behavior. Children are masters of creative and imaginative thinking, hallmarks of both Theta waves and an active, engaged subconscious mind. This suggests that Theta waves allow for easier communication between our conscious and subconscious minds.

The conscious, or awake, mind is able to understand, with a degree of controlled thought or observation, what is happening around us.

Our subconscious mind is the creative and imaginative aspect of our brain. The subconscious mind stores all our life experiences, beliefs, memories, skills, influences, and situations that are currently not in our conscious mind. Although we are not fully aware of all that it stores, the subconscious mind is such a powerful behavioral force that it can determine as much as 90% of our actions and feelings.

"The conscious mind may be compared to a fountain
playing in the sun and falling back into the great
subterranean pool of subconscious from which it rises."
—Sigmund Freud

In childhood, Theta predominance means that there is an unimpeded flow of impressions from our environment directly into the vast, undiscriminating storage banks of the subconscious mind. Thus, Theta waves have been identified as key in learning and memory. This is a powerful level from which behavior is created and to initiate change.

Neural Development

In addition to the exceptionally impressionable Delta and Theta brain-wave patterns in early childhood, our neural development also reflects the formation of our stimulus-reaction patterns, which are also known as our belief systems.

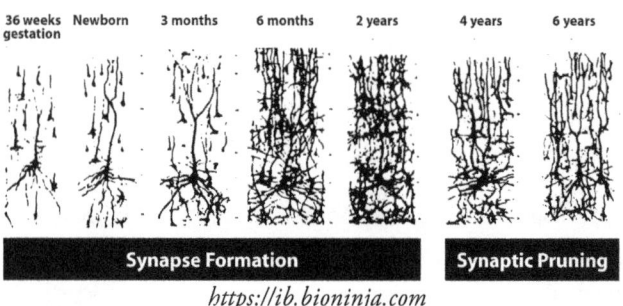

36 weeks gestation	Newborn	3 months	6 months	2 years	4 years	6 years

Synapse Formation   **Synaptic Pruning**

https://ib.bioninja.com

In the expansion and development of our neurons, as we can see in the chart above, a phenomenal neuron and synaptic proliferation occurs in early childhood. Think of the neuron bodies as towns on a map and the neuron tails (axon) as roads between the towns. Over the first few years, what emerges is urban sprawl: lots of neuron development and connections, each representing a stimulus-reaction pattern, each representing a behavior or habit, and each representing an ingraining of our belief systems.

The more habitually we react to an environmental stimulus, the more it reinforces specific neural connections in our brain.

Imagine a path between two towns. If given enough traffic, it will soon develop into a four-lane highway. Eventually, some of the side roads fall into disrepair and are rarely — if ever — used. In human brains, this is called "synaptic pruning." With synaptic pruning, our behavior begins to solidify by age seven.

Human Energy Field (HEF)

Interestingly, in addition to the influence of brain-wave patterns and neural expansion, there are profound developmental changes seen in the HEF, or aura, that occur around the age of seven.

The human body produces energy. This energy is seen in our body temperature, in our electrical nerve conductions, and in the chemical production of ATP. The human body also interacts with the energy that is present in the universe. The universe contains an exponential amount of energy. Our sun is just one small example of the energy that the universe produces. All these energies are vibrations.

Esoterically, the human body interfaces with this universal energy through the chakras. Chakra comes from the Sanskrit word for wheel. Chakras are energy vortices that allow the universal energy to interface with and nourish the body. There are seven major chakras – actually, seven pairs — front and back. They are shaped like a funnel. The small end of each funnel-like chakra is anchored into the spine. The universal energy flows into these chakras much like the whirlpool formed in your bath when you drain the tub. To an observer of the wider, open end of the funnel-like chakra, this whirlpool effect looks like a wheel spinning.

From the bottom of your spine to the top of your head, the chakras are numbered along the front of your body:

First: tip of the tailbone

Second: pubic bone

Third: solar plexus

Fourth: heart

Fifth: center of the throat

Sixth: middle of the forehead

Seventh: top of the head

Chakras two through six are paired with a corresponding chakra along the back of your body, like two funnels with the small ends facing each other.

According to Barbara Brennan's book *Hands of Light*, prior to the age of seven, "The field of the child is entirely open and vulnerable to the atmosphere in which he lives...The child's chakras are all open in the sense that there is no protective film over them which screens out the incoming influences.... At around the age of seven, a protective screen is formed over the chakra openings that filter out a lot of incoming influences.... This stage can be seen as the child grows and individuates... it is near the time of the dawning of reason."

Thus, we see how the mind-body connection is created.

The formation of the HEF and the development of energetic screens over the chakras correlate with the development of discretion. A child's ability to decide — or at least question — what influences shape his reality begins to solidify after the age of seven.

Prior to this stage — as seen in brain-wave frequency, neural development, and energetic field development — the child absorbs unfiltered, as though in a hypnotic state, without discretion, all the influences he is exposed to in his environment.

Information, experiences, perceptions, and influences are downloaded into the cellular fabric of the individual, much like the recording of a message or music onto tape.

There are actual physical, biochemical, cellular, energetic, and neural responses to all these influences whether the child experiences the stimuli through the senses of sight, sound, touch, smell, taste, or others.

4

Belief Systems

Your beliefs can be a prison system you've created for yourself.
But the door is not locked. You can come out of that.

—Amit Ray

Our perception — and therefore our definition — of reality arises from events, impressions, and influences which we are exposed to as children.

These experiences, once incorporated into our body-mind, become the foundation for what we believe the world is and how we believe the world functions. We define *belief* as being sure that a thing exists or that a thing is true. Our *belief systems*, or sets of mutually supportive truisms, are formed as a result of our reaction to thoughts, feelings, and actions in our childhood environment.

In the quest for mindfulness, an imperative point of awareness is, "I see what I believe."

"I see what I believe" creates the foundational connection between our beliefs and our behavior.

Belief Systems = Reality Diagram

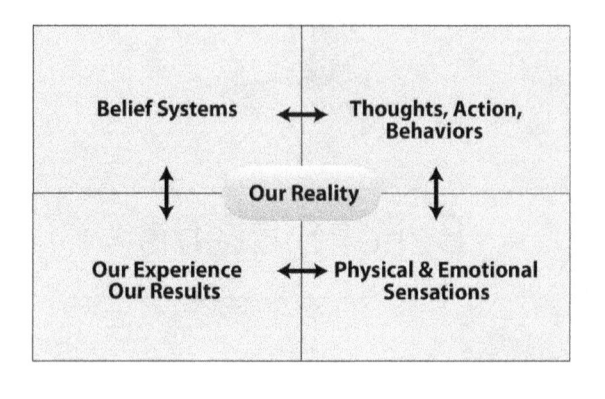

This diagram helps us visualize the belief-to-reality dynamic. Let's start in the box labeled Our Experience.

Imagine you are two years old. You're out for a walk in the park with your parents. Coming towards you is a large, shaggy, slobbering dog on a leash. Of course, most dogs will appear large to a two-year-old. This is a friendly dog, a bit exuberant, and as it approaches it begins to frolic. In its excitement, it lets out a couple of loud barks.

The physical sensation that the two-year-old experiences is one of tension. Your heart rate increases. Your breath becomes short. Emotionally, you may feel scared. You begin to cry and your parent, startled, yells at the dog.

In the diagram connecting belief systems and reality, you have moved from the Experience box on the bottom left into the Physical and Emotional Feelings box on the bottom right.

Your action is to recoil into the arms of your parent, figuring that is the best behavior to be safe. In the diagram, your action has now moved you into the Thoughts, Actions, Behaviors box in the top right.

This childhood experience led to physical and emotional sensations. Your physical and emotional feelings led to thoughts and actions. Your thoughts, feelings, and actions created a behavior. This process formed a specific neural pathway in your brain. That pathway became the basis of a habitual belief system. In this case, the belief system that formed was "big dogs are scary."

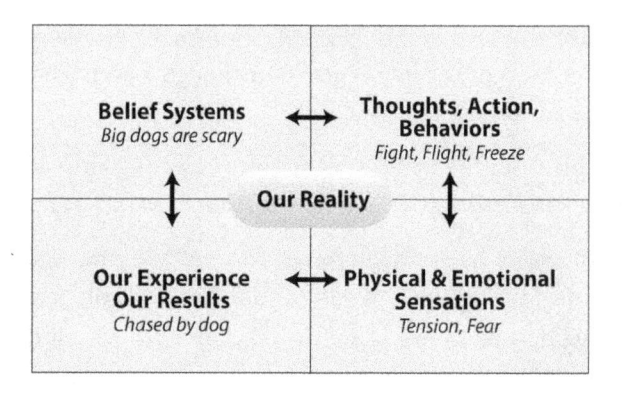

Now imagine you are ten years old. Walking home from school one day, you spot a big dog that you have never seen in the neighborhood. You get tense, perhaps without knowing why. Somewhere in your psyche, consciously or subconsciously, your belief system is reminding you that "big dogs are scary."

Your belief moves you into the classic fight, flight, or freeze stress response. After a paralyzing heart-pounding, breath-holding, mind-racing moment, you decide to make a run for it.

The dog, which had been paying absolutely no attention to you, now takes notice and chases you, barking.

You make it past the fence in your yard and slam the gate.

The dog, never really that interested in you to begin with, wanders off.

You are breathing hard. Your heart is going a thousand beats a minute. Your head is full with a loud buzz.

"Gosh," you say to yourself, "that was scary."

Your experience reinforces your belief.

Now imagine that at age two, in the park with your parents, a big, bouncy, slobbering dog comes along… but you have a different experience. You laugh. Something about that dog is funny. You feel relaxed, at ease. Your parents modeled your reaction and encourage the dog to come closer. They show you how to pet the dog. You feel the softness of the dog's ears. Your thoughts and behaviors are driven by curiosity.

In this case, the belief system you're creating through laying down a neural pathway is "big dogs are fun."

Then, years later, when you're ten and walking home from school, when the big dog wanders in your direction, you feel relaxed. It's no big deal. Curious where the dog came from, you decide to give him a name, Buster. You and Buster play fetch as you walk home together. The belief you developed at age two was that big dogs are fun. The experience you enjoy at age ten reinforces the belief.

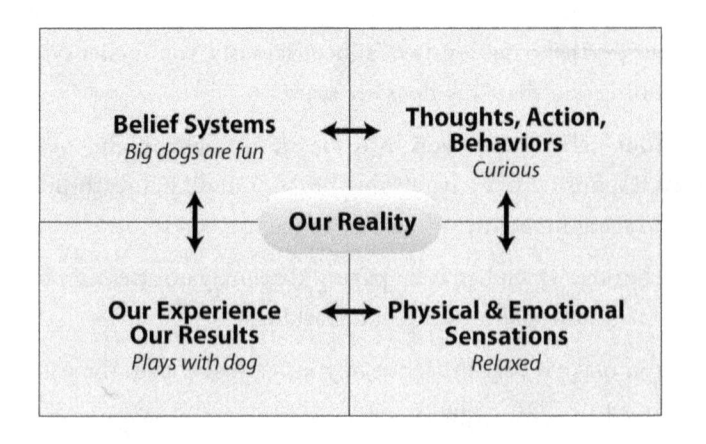

Belief systems can be as universal as "Big dogs are dangerous" or "Authority figures are scary." Belief systems also can be more specific, such as "I get more nurturing from women (mom) then men (dad)" or "When I express my needs, no one hears me."

Whatever universal and specific beliefs we form in childhood, those beliefs are based on what we call *child consciousness.*

The development of our consciousness is limited by our experiences as a child, the brain-wave frequency, our neural development, and characteristics of the HEF. Our consciousness is based on the concept that the world presents as all or nothing, because all information, experiences, perceptions, and influences are downloaded into our cellular fabric and our neural pathways, and directly into the vast, undiscriminating storage banks of the subconscious mind. "Big dogs are scary" becomes an absolute statement. As do such common belief systems as "all women are nurturing" and "I don't get a response when I express myself." All of these belief systems become absolute because we build and continuously reinforce the neural pathways.

These all-or-nothing statements build our foundational beliefs about what the world is and how it functions. Our belief systems thus determine how the world will present to us. And, because we've already decided how the world will present to us, our belief systems determine our experience of the world. Even if the objective world differs from what we subjectively believe the world to be.

All big dogs are scary. All women are nurturing. All men are _____. Any time we reach a conclusion or make an observation that follows the pattern "all _____ are_____," we know our child consciousness belief system is in play.

An adult consciousness — one that has the benefit of discretion, cognition, and experience — should be able to hold the concept that *some* big dogs are scary, and *some* big dogs are fun. The world is a scary place *at times*, and *at times* the world is a safe place.

But when we are very young, these absolute belief systems help us navigate and survive the foreign territory that all newborns encounter: life on earth. These belief systems are formed by how we have been programmed to react to events, not necessarily the events themselves. As children, it is essential for survival that these belief systems are in place. It is a way for the child consciousness to begin to make sense of the world and begin to create some pattern of consistency.

However, as we grow and develop adult consciousness, the belief systems we developed as young children still influence us. These belief systems — as adults, mostly residing in the vast warehouse of our subconscious — still direct our behavior.

Most all our actions and reactions occur reflexively, spontaneously. Our thoughts, feelings, and actions occur without the benefit of the awareness, intervention, and choice provided to us by the adult conscious mind's experiences. Much like an iceberg with 90% of its mass underwater, our subconscious mind holds 90% of our belief systems — that is, the stimulus-reaction patterns, behaviors, and habits that govern our day-to-day experiences of reality.

If you have ever uttered the words, "I promised myself that I wouldn't do that again," you are engaging with the force of your belief systems.

Any time you find yourself repeating behavior that, with a bit of thoughtful reflection, you would prefer not to repeat, you can be assured that your belief system's subconscious stimulus-reaction patterns are driving you.

But we are dedicated to our belief systems because they are the glue that holds our reality together.

As we have seen, belief systems are ingrained into our cellular, neuro-chemical, and energetic bodies. Belief systems — whether we acknowledge or are even aware of them — guide our behaviors, create our experiences, and define our reality. We hold fast to them.

In the quest for a mindful life, we strive to surrender to how things *are*, not how our belief systems tell us things *should be*.

This is not a destination we reach. It is a lifelong, daily practice. For when we challenge our beliefs, we challenge the very foundation of how we perceive and interact with the world around us and the people in it.

Accepting this challenge — and understanding that it is a challenge — is an essential element of transformational work and living a mindful life.

It takes a lot of courage to challenge our reality. Only by doing so can we fully embark on the journey of personal transformation.

Belief systems are limiting. Beyond judging whether they are good or bad, it is important to determine whether they are useful. This will allow us to integrate the effect of our belief systems into our personal transformation.

Mindfulness is about discovering, understanding, and incorporating balance. It is about broadening how we define ourselves. Our belief system about big dogs is not limiting until it becomes limiting — until it prevents us from the joy of engaging with a big, bouncy Buster.

Our belief systems become limiting when they limit us.

Our belief systems limit us when they prevent us from engaging with another because of what we believe about them, or prevent us from expressing our love because of how we believe love must be given or received, or prevent us from embracing the opportunities the universe provides us to grow.

Our belief systems can make us avoid all big dogs, whether they are real or metaphorical.

Practice:

Your belief systems are in play no matter how advanced, aware, enlightened, or spiritual you are. If you think you have conquered all your limiting beliefs, think again. Believing you have conquered your limiting beliefs is, of itself, a limiting belief.

In your journal, begin to identify your belief systems and the limits they impose on you by writing your responses to these challenges:

- Situations in which you make a judgment.
- Situations that make you feel tense.
- Situations when you suffer an irrational fear.
- Situations when you demand someone, or something be a particular way.
- Situations to which you respond, "All _____ are _____."
- Situations that make you realize you're doing something you promised you would no longer do.

PART TWO

The Three Inquiries

5

Creating Our Own Reality

If two such physical theories or models accurately predict the same events, one cannot be said to be more real than the other; rather, we are free to use whichever model is most convenient.

—Stephen Hawkins and Leonard Mlodinow

THE AIR WAS chilly as the high, thin clouds filtered the sun's warmth. It was Saturday, early spring, and we were undeterred as we headed into the woods. Skirting the last patches of snow, sticking to dry ground, clumps of weeds, and bare logs, we soon came to the swollen creek.

My friend approached the bank, hesitated, and looked back at me with a clever grin.

"I'll believe it when I see it," I yelled. Part fact, part dare.

My friend, spurred on by both the adventure and the challenge of my words, scrambled from bank to log to rock to bank in a gravity-defying hop, skip, and jig across the creek. When his heels splashed just shy of dry land, he had defied reason and somehow made it to the other side.

"I'll believe it when I see it" is a common phrase driven by the skeptic in us. My friend claimed he could cross that silt-grey creek without falling in. I doubted it. And I didn't believe it was possible until I witnessed the event.

In the quest for mindfulness, what if — just for fun — we flip that phrase: "I'll see it when I believe it."

Or, even more to the point, "I see what I believe."

The Development and Precepts of Reality

I see what I believe, and the precepts of how we perceive reality — as well as the development of our belief systems — begins prior to birth. It peaks in our early childhood and becomes increasingly set in place as we age.

As children, we react to the stimuli in our environment. A repetitive stimulus with repetitive reactions lays the foundation for our repetitive patterns. These become our habits. A habit is any behavior that we repeat regularly. For the most part, the reasons we repeat behaviors are subconscious.

A *belief system* is a conceptual framework that we develop to make sense of our world. We develop a patterned reaction to stimuli. We develop a particular belief around a particular stimulus. Pulling your hand away after touching a hot stove is a particular stimulus-reaction pattern.

Stimulus-reaction patterns become ingrained in our physical body as well as our psyche. In the hot stove example, it might take only one experience to develop the belief that hot stoves are painful and dangerous. Yet from that belief, we develop a lifelong habit. Not only do we avoid hot stoves, but we cautiously hold our hand above the stove top and check the knobs to make sure the stove isn't hot.

The more frequently we experience the stimulus-reaction pattern, the more habitual our behavior becomes. Our physical, mental, and emotional reaction patterns are driven by our belief systems and they guide our behavior throughout our lives.

Using the Mundane to Enhance our Soul's Journey

Belief systems are continuously at play in our dance with reality.

Transformational work demands that we use the mundane world and details of our life experience to reveal our incarnational tasks — our soul's journey — also known as our Great Quest. In this way, using the mundane will enhance our soul's journey as we expand our awareness into the highest evolutionary potential our life has to offer.

To discover the patterns of our stimulus-reaction belief systems, we can examine the details of any mundane experience we have. This mundane experience will reveal to us valuable insight into our Great Quest.

Once we acquire a stimulus-reaction pattern, it will always exist.

Even though I know my stimulus-reaction responses, it does not imply that I can transcend the way I react when confronted with this, or any, stimulus-reaction pattern. Reactions, because they are hardwired and cellularly embedded into our psyche, will always affect our physical, mental, and emotional bodies. For example:

Physical — Fight, flee, or freeze.

Mental — Figure out what to do.

Emotional — Accept that fear reactions will always occur.

These reactions are also karmic. This means that certain behaviors in this lifetime are brought forward from a previous life simply because we have yet to heal or develop beyond them.

The Takeaway

The transformational question becomes: does this stimulus-reaction pattern last several lifetimes, a lifetime, a year, an hour, or a nanosecond?

The gift of mindful awareness means we can notice our own stimulus-reaction patterns.

If we can observe them, we can respond to them.

And responding to them allows us to shorten the amount of time we are locked into the reactive habits of a belief system that limits the pursuit of our Great Quest.

6

Allowing an Experience to be Valid and Useful

Life will give you whatever experience is most helpful for the evolution of your consciousness.
How do you know this is the experience you need?
Because this is the experience you are having at the moment.

—Eckhart Tolle

IN OUR QUEST for a mindful life, it is essential that we allow experiences that make no logical sense to inform and expand our perception.

I was in the midst of a craniosacral somato-emotional release session (SER). This is a hands-on modality that works by releasing restrictions in the connective tissues of our body. Somatic refers to the body. Emotional refers to our body's ability to hold emotional experiences in the tissues. Hence, somato-emotional release works to reveal locked-in patterns of the mind-body connection.

As the therapist released some connective tissue restrictions around my rib cage and liver, a scene began to unfold in my mind. I saw myself as a seven-month-old resting in this large folding play-pen made of dark green fabric mesh. It was summer. I felt the warm air on my skin. I was at my grandparent's house on the Jersey shore. I heard pleasant noise in the background — comforting sounds of voices and birds, the soft rustle of the breeze.

I lay on my side, quiet. My breath came in short spurts, more holding and tense than relaxed. There was this discomfort — an ache, a pressure — around my rib cage and liver.

A girl, teenage years, hovered over me. She slowly moved away. Somehow, I knew she was in charge of watching me — perhaps a babysitter or friend of the family there to help.

The scene rolled back in time just a bit. I realized she was the one that had caused the pressure and pain in my abdomen by push-ing forcibly on my belly.

The pain I was experiencing in the somato-emotional release session was the pain I had felt at that moment in the playpen.

Rolling back in time again, I saw myself as a baby expressing my needs in the way babies do -making sounds, crying, and gurgling. In this vision, this movie running across the screen in my mind, I began to understand where this pain came from and the events surrounding it.

The pain and emotional experience of my infancy were locked away in my body's connective tissue until that SER session. This teenage girl had pushed on my belly to quiet me. After all, a babysit-ter with a fussy, crying baby must not be doing her job right.

This experience I had as a baby was the beginning of the belief/ image I have carried my whole life. It's a belief that says, "If I express myself — and especially if I express my needs — it will cause me pain."

I could take this story a bit further and say, "If I express my needs — especially with females — I will not be safe, I will be hurt, and my needs will not be met."

Of course, it could be argued that this entire story has absolutely no basis in fact. Confirming this event happened might be impossible. My memory could be a complete fabrication.

Yet the power of this experience is not dependent on it being *true*. The power of this experience resides solely in whether I allow this experience to be *valid*. Do I allow it to have meaning and relevance, or do I dismiss it? Generally, we are quick to dismiss experiences that fall outside of our comfort zone.

One of the greatest impediments to expanding our insight, intuition, gut feelings, or guidance as a tool for mindfulness is the ease with which we discount uncomfortable or discomforting experiences.

It is exceedingly difficult to create new patterns in our life if we do not allow odd experiences to affect us. It would have been easy to put aside the mental movie of my childhood experience. It's easy to dismiss such memories as unimportant fantasies. The memory and the experience certainly made no rational sense.

From that moment in the therapy room, I had a clear understanding and kinesthetic experience of a belief system. The belief had been actively alive in my subconscious. It had guided — was guiding — my behavior. It was a belief system woven into the tapestry of my life: If I believe that it is unsafe or painful to express myself, and that pattern is locked into my physical body and emotional psyche, that belief system clearly limits my ability to be expressive or state my needs.

Personal transformation cannot occur without an understanding of our subconscious belief systems and the behaviors that arise from them.

We cannot uncover and discover our belief systems until we allow synchronistic events to be valid. A synchronistic event is a coincidence that appears to have no connection to your experience, yet potentially holds great meaning and significance.

Something being valid is not necessarily the same as something being true. A *valid* experience is one that is at once relevant and meaningful. Not being vested in whether my experience as a seven-month-old is *true* allows me the freedom to see how the experience might be valid and therefore useful.

That experience, like any experience, becomes relevant and meaningful because I allow it to be so.

If I dismiss that experience as too farfetched to be true, then I dismiss the gift of the insight. And insight always carries the potential to be one of our most transformational and empowering tools.

Seen from another angle — and perhaps more comfortable for the left brain, rational mind — I might chalk up the experience as simply being a metaphor.

Either way, it still has the power to be valid. Therefore, it has the power to enlighten me.

To see if I can incorporate this dynamic into mindfulness and transformation, I explore the following two steps:

1. I allow an insightful, odd, or "that makes no sense" experience to be valid.

2. I decide if this valid experience is useful.

So, the question becomes, "How do I make this valid experience useful?"

In this transformational moment, I have come to a fork in the road, so to speak. If I discount what has just transpired, I will tend to stay with the familiar patterns that have defined my behavior my entire life. I will choose not to express myself because I believe it will be both painful and it won't make any difference.

Opening to an experience that makes no sense drops my awareness into the right brain. That's the territory of the subconscious. By entering through that doorway, I am able to explore — and ultimately challenge — the belief systems that drive my behavior.

We have to know what drives behavior to get to the root of healing our limiting patterns. This is certainly different from the common therapeutic approach of behavior modification. The general approach of behavior modification is, roughly, "I just won't do that anymore."

How successful has that approach been for you?

Evaluating valid experiences to decide if they're useful is a deeper, more transformational approach to living mindfully. Here is another example:

I was at a Monroe Institute training retreat. My group was engaged in exploring expanded states of consciousness through guided visualization. We listened to specific sounds or music that can entrain specific brain waves. This approach enables meditation into very expanded states of consciousness. After each ninety-minute solo session, we would share our experiences.

One participant of the group expressed continual frustration because all he ever experienced was a sense of relaxation and a journey that was nothing but darkness. For him, this was not a valid experience. Whatever he'd hoped for — light, color, angelic beings — did not manifest. His belief was that, unless his experience looked a particular way, it was not a valid experience.

At that point, his opportunity to transform himself had stopped.

Yet consider the possibility that, had he been able to allow "nothing but darkness" to be valid, it could have opened him deeper into another experience from which any number of infinite possibilities could arise. Hearkening to the wisdom of the Tao te Ching:

Darkness within darkness, the gateway to all understanding.

The goal of a mindful life is to expand and allow experiences that come to us to be valid. This is especially true for experiences that don't fit into how we believe things should be.

Now this becomes useful:

I have a craniosacral treatment. A story unfolds within my internal vision. I enter my vast subconscious databanks. An insight into a foundational belief gets evoked.

The belief is, "If I express my needs, I will not be safe, I will be hurt, and the need will not be met."

Suffice to say, a belief such as this could affect relationships. It could limit my ability to be forthright and expressive of my needs. I could project onto others a silent demand that they should meet my unspoken needs and that they should know what they are — even if I don't!

In this example, the answer to the question about the validity of my experience is - yes. Setting aside the argument that it may or may not be true, my experience can be useful because it allows me to consciously challenge my limiting patterns.

By allowing the experience to be valid, I am able to understand the root of my behavior. From that understanding, that *awareness*, I can begin to heal. I can begin to witness this pattern and to hold compassion for the childhood trauma that set this behavior in motion. I can, using the gift of insight, use adult consciousness to make a choice.

This is the hallmark of enlightenment.

I can, with courage, take the risk to express myself and state my needs.

A mindful life begins with a seemingly simple fact:

Awareness can bring light and knowledge to a previously darkened aspect of our psyche.

If we allow it to emerge, awareness begins to challenge the hard-wired, neurological, cellular, and energetic patterns that created our behavioral habits. As we become aware of these patterns and witness ourselves in our relationships, we create the opportunity to become more empowered as to the choices we make in life.

Practice:

Take a moment to sit quietly. Center yourself by breathing gently and deeply into your lower abdomen. Relax your throat and shoulders. Listen to the sounds around you. Allow yourself to get lost in your breath and what you hear. Relax your mind and your body and without effort connect the two.

Make a vow that you will allow an odd, unusual, or "too far-fetched to be true" thought, intuition, or experience be valid.

Commit an hour, or part of your day, or even the whole day to this vow.

Witness how frequently you dismiss or discount the synchronistic, odd, or "that makes no sense" events in your day.

The universe offers guidance in the most mundane and simple ways. For example, I went to the hardware store to buy some cleaning supplies. As I walked down the aisle, I noticed a pair of high-quality scissors on sale. "Hmm," I thought, "those scissors would be great, but I am after cleaning supplies." I got home and found my daughter searching for scissors for an art project. None could be found.

The Takeaway

It could be as simple as allowing that odd intuition to be valid and seeing how that affects your mindful journey through the day.

7

Going Beyond Creating Our Own Reality

Reality is merely an illusion,
albeit a very persistent one.

—Albert Einstein

WE ARE DEDICATED to our belief systems because they are the glue that holds our reality together.

As we have seen, belief systems are ingrained into our cellular, biochemical, and energetic bodies. They guide our behavior, create our experiences, and define who we are. We hold fast to them.

In the quest for a mindful life we strive to be aware of our belief systems. We notice their limiting effects. We challenge them. From this place of empowered, curious questioning, we make a choice

— the hallmark of enlightenment — about how we want to be in the world.

This is not a destination we reach, but a lifelong practice. When we challenge our reality, we challenge the very foundation of how we perceive and interact with the world around us and the people in it. This is an essential element of transformational work and in living a mindful life.

It takes great courage to challenge our reality. But only by doing so can we fully embark on the journey of personal transformation.

The Belief Creates the Experience
The Experience Reinforces the Belief

"I create my own reality" is a familiar paradigm. A paradigm is a group of ideas about how something should be done, made, or thought about.

The paradigm "I create my own reality" is based on the concept that — whether we know it or not, whether we are proactive or reactive — we are responsible for creating the experiences in our life.

This paradigm is easy to appreciate when things are going our way.

The paradigm is significantly more difficult to accept when life is traumatic, overwhelming, or painful.

To go beyond creating our own reality, we must challenge the way we believe the world is. Previously, we saw that — in essence — we experience the world as we *believe* it to be, not necessarily how it *objectively* is.

It was one of those hazy, lazy late-winter Sundays of just hanging around the house. The breakfast crumbs and dishes were still on the table. The laundry was still piled on the couch. Other Sunday chores lingered here and there. All would be attended to in due time.

I was in the midst of a lively discussion with my partner. And by discussion, I mean it was argument. I don't recall the details of it or how it started. But, after about 45 minutes, I realized this particular discussion was exactly like every other argument I'd ever had with a partner. It felt the same. It sounded the same. It carried the same hallmarks.

Those hallmarks included:

I felt misunderstood.

I felt frustrated.

I felt physically tense.

Busy defending myself, I sent subtle verbal arrows towards my partner. I say subtle because I wore the mask that claimed, "I'm OK. I'm calm. I'm rational. You're the one who's upset."

I told myself, "They must like to argue. Otherwise, it wouldn't be happening. I clearly don't want to spend my time arguing, so it's not me causing this. It's them."

The belief system at play in this repetitive relational dynamic said, "If I share what I think and how I feel, I will be misunderstood." The belief system continued: "The more I express myself, the more likely it will create conflict."

Well, of course!

That's what was happening. I was misunderstood. There was conflict. That's not my belief system — that's reality!

Practice:

In the dance of human relationships, there are familiar and repetitive themes that surface in our relational arguments. The themes I mentioned may be personally familiar to you. You may have other themes that thread through your relationships.

Here are my themes. I blamed them for:

- Creating conflict.

- How the argument made me feel.

- Wasting my time in strife.

- Not understanding me.

Reflect on your themes and write them in your journal.

The insight

When I don't like how reality plays out, I blame someone else.

That blame — no matter how subtle my demeanor — has the unintended consequence of infuriating my partner. It perpetuates the exact reality I claim I don't want: the feeling of being misunderstood, tense, and defensive.

That is my habitual and repetitive limiting relationship pattern. And it's common. How often have you been blamed, either directly or through inference, during an argument? How does it make you feel? Infuriated, perhaps?

Take a few moments and respond to this prompt in your journal:

This is how I feel when I am blamed: _____

Our belief systems are powerful. They create the foundations of our reality. On a subconscious level, we are dedicated to making sure our reality is true because if our reality is true, our beliefs must be true.

Driven by this subconscious dedication, we will — through our actions — evoke in another specific behaviors that prove our belief systems *are* our reality.

Those behaviors will confirm our beliefs about the other, about us, about relationships, about everyone, about everything.

If my belief system states that when I share my feelings I will be misunderstood, I will make sure that my partner misunderstands what I am saying. This way, my belief system — the constructs and foundation of my reality — stays true.

"Wow," I thought, "here I am again."

A patient universe offered me yet another opportunity. An opportunity to pause, to become the witness — the unattached observer, the nonjudgmental participant — to this most mundane of all events — an argument with my partner. An opportunity to blow open my reality and to garner insight into my greater soul's journey.

An opportunity, with grace and effort and mindfulness, to challenge my belief systems and shift my reality.

Challenging the Paradigm

To engage a mindful life — to proactively experience transformation and go beyond the habitual creations of our reality — it is essential that we challenge our paradigms.

All paradigms have their limitations. They are, by definition, only a construct or theory of how something is or should be. The moment we define a thing or come to a conclusion about it, that thing then becomes limited.

Knowing that, and curiously searching for a broader interaction and understanding of our reality, allows us to break the chains of a dogmatic life.

The more we challenge our limiting definitions and conclusions about a person, place, thing, or idea, the more empowered we become. We free ourselves and others from the confines of knowing or defining how something should be done, made, or thought about.

At the highest level, the quest of transformational work and mindful living is to go beyond the paradigms that define us and limit our life experiences.

More specifically, there are three inquiries that will help challenge the "I create my own reality" paradigm. After we learn them, we can apply these inquiries to all paradigms.

The Three Inquiries

The three inquiries are:

1. Is this paradigm true? That I create my own reality?

2. *Why* am I creating this reality?

3. Because I am creating this experience, can I go beyond the first two inquiries into a more empowered life?

The first inquiry challenges whether the paradigm is true.

"I create my own reality."

Is this paradigm true?

Do you fully believe that you create your own reality? The universe does not require that we hold this paradigm factual. If we do not give credence to it, then that, in and of itself, is a paradigm.

Not believing a paradigm is a paradigm. We do not have to believe something for it to be true. We don't even have to understand something for it to have an application in our life. We still engage with our reality, which continues to engage the physical laws of the universe. We just engage with it from that particular point of view.

Through the years in my private practice as an acupuncturist, I have had many patients tell me that they didn't believe in acupuncture. This conversation invariably happened just prior to the first needle insertion during their first treatment.

I always found that curious. I thought, "How can you not believe something that exists and that can have such a profound effect on the human body?"

Early in my practice, I was dedicated to explaining the *why* of acupuncture. I was attached to convincing my patients that they should believe in the power of acupuncture. I was full of facts and subtle demands that they "get it."

After a few years in practice, I began to witness an interesting phenomenon. I observed that acupuncture was effective regardless of whether the patient believed it. Patients who believed in acupuncture created a different relationship to their experience of the treatment than patients who did not. The experiences of both kinds of patients were equally valid. I saw a difference in the levels of active engagement in both groups, but it made little difference in the level of both groups' success.

A mindful life is one of active engagement. It's open to a wide range of possibilities, regardless of the outcome.

Any one of us can live successfully without consciously engaging the paradigm "I create my reality." We can enjoy life's riches and accept life's sorrows without ever engaging the paradigm. It becomes important only if we pay attention to it and make it a useful aspect of our life.

When we actively and consciously engage the paradigm that we create our own reality, our experiences reflect the truth of that paradigm. For Person One, further exploration of this topic becomes a moot point. Person One continues to live successfully, enjoying life's riches and accepting its sorrows.

For Person Two, who believes in the proactive "I create my reality," it opens the floodgate of opportunities that will enhance active engagement in personal transformation and move Person Two into the slipstream of awareness towards a rendezvous with a mindful life.

The second inquiry challenges us to understand *why* we are creating this particular reality.

Why can evoke childlike curiosity. *Why* inherently asks, "For what reason or purpose?"

This is rich territory for self-awareness and exploration.

Why allows us, without bias, to witness the unfolding life around us. It can evoke contemplation, a place of stillness, an opening for a-ha moments. Holding *why* in this context opens to deep, useful, and life-changing insight.

It is a *why* not looking so much for an answer but for a pause, for a witnessing of the moment, for a reflective view of our current experience.

The question *why* can also lead us into a maze of action that produces lots of work but few results. Why can imply irritation or blame:

"Why did you paint it that color?"

"Why didn't you call me?"

"Why don't you share your feelings?"

In this context. the use of *why* masks some irritation or resentment in a socially acceptable manner. In this context, asking *why* is equivalent to blaming:

"I blame you for painting it a color I don't like."

"I blame you for not calling me and leaving me waiting."

"I blame you for how I feel scared and alone when you don't share your feelings."

Why becomes our way to place fault on the other for actions and behaviors we don't like. "Why are you doing this?" and "Why is this happening?" commonly arise when our experience or reality doesn't match our expectations.

Why, when used in this context, is a demand on others to be responsible for our life and feelings.

Practice:

Any time we use *why* in the context of something we don't like, we use *why* to blame.

This is easy to observe in our day-to-day life. Just witness your use of *why*. Become aware of the energy and intent behind it. With a curious *why*, there will be no irritation or demand in your physical or emotional body. You are open-hearted, curious, childlike. On the other hand, if you are irritated, tense, or have a demand when you ask *why*, then you are in blame.

Draw a line down the middle of a page in your journal. At the top of one column, write Curiosity. In the other column, write Blame.

Spend some time — an hour, or even a whole day — noticing your use of *why* and the energy that accompanies it.

Put check marks in each column as you use *why* as either curiosity or as blame.

Reflect on this experience.

Our Lesson

There are times when we blame others under the guise of *why*. There are times when we blame ourselves:

"Why does this always happen to me?"

"I must be doing something wrong."

"What is the lesson I am supposed to learn?"

That last one is my all-time favorite. We blame ourselves for not knowing *why* our experiences are so dissonant, and for not learning our lessons. If only we understood *why* this was happening, we would change our behavior. Our changed behavior would give us different experiences.

But if our experiences don't change, we conclude. "There must really be something wrong with me." In that context, the innocent place and curious wonder of *why* is hijacked and becomes an avenue for self-blame.

In well-intended — but sorely misplaced — action, we embark on a desperate search for The Answer. We hope it will give us enough understanding to propel us out of life's repetitive patterns. This becomes our personal search for understanding *why*.

This is the holy grail of trying to figure out *why* our life is as it is.

We fall into the trap of focusing our efforts on trying to understand our life patterns instead of transforming ourselves so we can shift these life patterns. We fool ourselves into thinking that we are gaining awareness through our efforts. Frequently, we are doing nothing more than following the patterns that define our habits and our limits.

Trying to understand *why* beyond curious, innocent seeking becomes a shadow piece of blame. It prevents us from generating enough energy to propel us out of the spin cycle of trying to get it — as in, "As soon as I get (or they) get it, then _____ will be different."

The *why* of blame burns critical energy that we need to go beyond the belief systems that define us. It distracts us from the hard work of getting past the paradigms that limit our life experiences.

There is the potential to become more invested in just working on our stuff than actually transforming ourselves. We fall down that slippery slope of pseudo-awareness because we appear, by all internal efforts and outward action, as though we are working on it. We assume that if we are working on it, we are living a mindful life.

We fall into the mistake of defining ourselves by the effort we put forth.

This shadow piece keeps us in a perpetual cycle of creating a repetitive experience. And we do so under the guise of making progress towards enlightenment!

When someone says, "I am responsible for creating my reality," what they likely mean is, "I am aware of my patterns, my creations, my reality."

But being aware of a pattern does not change that pattern.

For example, I had a patient in my practice. She was bright, engaged, and intelligent. She was dedicated to growth, learning, and searching for a deeper understanding of her life and relationships. She struggled with a specific reactive relational pattern pertaining to "feeling small and disempowered" with men. One day, she told me, "I've been working on this for 15 years."

Her heartfelt statement revealed the depth of her dedication to herself and her unrelenting desire to live a mindful life. Relationships can be the crucible for personal growth. She is certainly not alone in her endeavor to create relationships that are more rewarding.

Yet there is a possibility that "I've been working on this for 15 years" places her on that slippery slope of "As soon as I understand why, then I can transform it."

We can fool ourselves into thinking that we are making progress and gaining awareness. We can think we are working towards transformation when we are, in a clever and sophisticated way, recycling our habitual and limiting life patterns.

"I've been working on this for 15 years" was a statement about her awareness. It was not a statement about her empowerment. It was not a statement that gave her the opportunity to respond differently to "feeling small and disempowered" with men for more than 15 years.

Transformation

Rarely is transformation complicated. Instead, we make it complicated.

We make it complicated because that gives us something to do. We busy ourselves with books, classes, workshops, therapists, and healthcare providers. These activities engage us. They can open us to deep and profound awareness.

This can be a very useful thing. The greater our awareness, the greater our foundation to challenge and expand our reality. We are totally dedicated to our reality because it is the glue that holds our world together.

Awareness is the soil in which we cultivate mindfulness, transformation, and enlightenment.

The Ability to Respond

But by any measure, awareness is not the endpoint.

It is limiting to conflate awareness with enlightenment. Awareness is the essential first step on the road to living a mindful life. *Responsiveness* is the essential second step. Being responsive is what allows us to consciously change our limiting life patterns.

After we've broadened our awareness, what comes next? Are we *able to respond* to our newly broadened awareness? What is our mindful obligation to this awareness? What is our responsibility to it in some great soulful way?

Let's be excruciatingly literal for a moment and define responsibility as "response ability." Responsibility means having the ability to respond. With this understanding of the term, we see that being aware and being responsible — being able to respond — to that awareness are two separate steps on the journey.

Awareness builds the foundation from which we can consciously respond.

When we engage in the *why* of our life, it is essential to distinguish between the *why* of curiosity and the *why* of blame.

To stay on the path, focus on the curious, childlike *why* that deepens our journey. This is the *why* that gives us a pause in the unfolding dynamics of the present moment.

Avoid the *why* that masks blame and keeps us wandering the maze of "working on it."

The third inquiry challenges us to go beyond the first two inquiries into a more empowered life.

"I am creating this" is a cellular statement. A cellular statement is an experience of insight that we can feel in our bodies on a cellular level.

When we experience something cellularly, or make a cellular statement, we feel it kinesthetically. A shift occurs in our body. We feel a sensation. It could be warmth, relaxation, or breath change. We feel less push or pull. We feel more neutral, more grounded.

Without fail, when I observe someone say, "I am creating this," a smile spreads across their face. When I ask them about their smile, they will respond that they feel more empowered.

We can use the three inquiries to go beyond creating our own reality in any of our relational dynamics. That's what happened to me on that lazy Sunday as my partner and I had a discussion that really was an argument.

First, I asked myself, "Is this paradigm true?"

"I create my own reality." Is this paradigm true?

If I truly believe this paradigm, I cannot blame the other for my experience of reality. Period. If I am creating it, it cannot be anyone else's fault.

So, do I really believe this paradigm even though I don't like my reality? I always thought I believed this paradigm. Check that off the list — I mean, I'm an enlightened, progressive kind of guy.

And yet, even though I fully believed it, I still blamed my partner for the pain and strife I was experiencing.

I believed that I create my reality, but I also believed I was not creating that reality. My partner was. I was blaming.

I believed I was doing the best I could. Why didn't my partner understand? I was playing the role of victim.

I believed the argument emerged from my partner's problem — not my problem. In addition to blaming, I was separating myself from my partner.

The paradigm that I create my reality is easy to believe when my life is going great. It's much easier to believe it when everything is smooth and fun and easy than when something (or everything) isn't.

In living a mindful life, we must question how much we really believe our paradigms, even one as common as I create my reality. Any time we find ourselves in circumstances that are traumatic or painful — any time the dynamic of blame is in play — is an opportunity the universe grants us to question our belief in the truth of our paradigms.

If we truly believe we create our reality — if we lay claim to a mindful life, if our awareness becomes fertile ground for our ability to respond — then how can we ever blame another for our experiences?

Second, I asked myself, "Why am I creating this?"

When I am in the middle of conflict and I ask *why*, the question rarely comes from that curious, childlike place of exploration. It comes from a place of blame: "This sucks! Why am I creating this?" *Why* fell right into blame.

In my Sunday argument with my partner, what I really asked myself was, "Why is *she* creating this?" Moments of curious *why* can occur during conflict, but — honestly — it is nearly impossible to ask the curious, innocent *why* in those situations.

Yet, if through intention and the grace of the universe, we are able to pause and become an observer — and not a player — of the dynamic we're in, a curious *why* will have space to arise.

The curious, innocent *why* will much more easily occur when the physical, emotional, and mental aspects of our psyche are open, relaxed, and undefended. It will more easily occur in moments of true contemplation. It may arise at a point after we free ourselves of strife.

At that point, the curious *why* can deepen our insight.

Third, I asked myself, "Because I am creating this experience, can I go beyond the first two inquiries into a more empowered life?"

I was in that kitchen, in the middle of that argument. Again.

I was repeating the familiar, uncomfortable experience of my reality — the reality I created — when a curious *why* prompted a life-changing insight. It was no less illuminating then the ray of sunlight breaking through the clouds.

For the first time ever, I perceived that my search for *why* — my yearning to answer the question, "What lesson is the universe trying to teach me?" — had trapped me in a maze. The maze was my never-ending search for the elusive holy grail of trying to get it. I'd spent years trying to figure out and understand this all-too-familiar relational pattern.

I had spent years "working on it."

At that moment, I realized — I knew, with startling simplicity — that I created it. I said to myself, "I am creating this." No charge. No blame. I didn't debate the validity or truth of "I am creating this." I didn't go into the briar patch of *why*, also known as blame. There was no blurring into the morphic new age, slippery-slope paradigm of "I create my reality, what is my lesson, what do I need to learn, why is this happening blah, blah, blah."

I said it to myself again, "I am creating this." Again, no charge. No blame.

I actually felt a physical release of my intense internal tension. I felt lighter. I felt empowered. In fact, I started to smile because the actual conflict in the moment seemed so ludicrous. It was as if I was an actor in some Felliniesque play. I could recite my lines, as the habitual script of my belief system had programmed me... or I could improvise a new behavior.

Nourished by a new awareness that allowed me the ability to respond to this all-too-familiar dynamic in a different way, I was able at that moment to make a conscious choice.

A conscious choice — the brightest of all hallmarks on the serpentine path of enlightenment.

I felt strangely present and yet unattached to the dynamic. I felt my body/mind pause. I became the witness to myself, my partner, and the argument that was unfolding before me. I felt liberated, patient, understanding, and even joyful. A smile crossed my face.

It did not go over well with my partner.

But at least my heart began to open. I could see myself and my partner as soulful beings that existed beyond the personalities we create to live in this manifest world.

"I am creating this." The statement must be made from the witness role. The witness role is the nonjudgmental, open, observer role. In the witness role, you notice what you notice without attachment. You make no conclusions about what it all means.

The witness role is empowering. It is the essence of presence. "Without attachment" does not mean separation. The open observer role fully participates with curiosity. Curiosity creates the opening for the infusion of wisdom.

Try this. From this witness role, make this statement:

I am creating this experience.

It's simple. As an observer — not as a participant — try it again:

I am creating it.

How does that feel?

You might feel something in your body: fullness, release of tension, warmth, stillness.

What you are most likely to feel is a sense of neutrality, a sense of empowerment, and — here is the best part — a profound inability to blame yourself or anyone else for your life.

As you do this, you have entered new territory. You've become totally responsible for your experiences. You've assumed responsibility because you are conscious of your ability to respond. You can respond to the present moment with awareness instead of reacting from habit.

You have become empowered. You have the choice, the option, and the ability to respond.

Living a mindful life is not about falling prey to the siren song of having to understand *why* or the allure of seeking awareness as an end point.

Living a mindful life rests in our ability to witness without blame and create a conscious response to the awareness we gather on this journey through life.

Practice: The Three Inquiries

1. **Is this paradigm true?**

A paradigm is a perspective or set of ideas. Choose one, such as:

- I create my own reality.
- A marriage is a commitment "till death do we part".
- My sense of self is dependent on my income.
- If I eat organic foods, I won't get sick.

- A paradigm that challenges or troubles you.

Write the paradigm you've chosen in your journal.

2. **Why am I creating this reality?**

This is the curious *why* that deepens the process of self-discovery and insight. It is free of blame, judgment, and the demand that we find *the* answer.

Questions that can help you with the Second Inquiry and deepen insight include:

- What's here now? This is the witness role.

- How does it impact me? This is part of taking inventory.

- In what way does this mundane experience support my soul's evolutionary journey? Small, repetitive events often are clues on the path to discovering our Great Quest.

The universe might be granting you the opportunity to practice patience, listening, forgiveness, compassion, courage, independence, trust, or another valuable quality.

- What is the universe letting me practice?

Record your thoughts in your journal.

3. **Because I am creating it, can I go beyond the first two inquiries into a more empowered life?**

Out beyond ideas of wrongdoing and right-doing there is a field. I'll meet you there. When the soul lies down in that grass, the world is too full to talk about.

—Rumi

Here we make a quantum leap. The first two inquiries build the foundation we need to go beyond creating our reality. Given that foundation, we are able to step into a more empowered life.

There are no excuses here.

There is only presence and the ability to respond to our awareness.

The manifestation of this quantum leap, as is true for all great and small transformational moments, is not of habit.

It takes courage. It takes vulnerability. It takes practice — practice to move from who we are to who we get to be.

The intention and empowerment of going beyond the creation of our reality is summed up in the mantra:

I am creating this.

Consider this mantra from a witness, heartfelt, grounded place:

I am creating this.

Consider this in your next moment of angst, strife, or discord:

I am creating this.

Consider it when paradigms collide, when reality shakes. Consider it when you notice a routine or habit is something you'd prefer to abandon.

I am creating this.

Mundane experiences support your soul's journey. Those kinds of transformative journeys take lots of practice.

In your day to day life, the universe will give you opportunities just as it did in my example with my partner. The opportunity is to practice going beyond creating our own reality.

As part of the mantra "I am creating this," thank the universe for its patient participation in your evolution.

Now you get to practice.

PART THREE

Moving from Reaction to Response

8

The Transformational Moment

And you? When will you begin that long journey into yourself?

—Rumi

IT WAS SNOWING and snowing hard. Driving over this winding mountain pass always required a fair amount of attention and a modicum of respect. In the early morning dark, as the headlights reflected the mesmerizing dance of large, fast-falling flakes, the pass was demanding a great deal of respect.

Lulled by the beauty of the falling snow and those tall, frosted, sentry-like evergreens that lined the narrow two-lane road, I pushed aside that twinge of anxiety that stirred in my belly. Our Volvo was handling well, and I chose to say nothing to my brother, who — pushed by our late start — was driving faster than I thought the conditions called for.

As we approached a long bend in the road, that heavy solid Volvo did well to navigate the curve. Until it didn't.

The steering wheel turned the car's wheels, but the car — as though pushed by an unseen force — remained on its straight-line course.

In that moment, my sense of linear time suspended itself. Time unfolded simultaneously in a way that was both surprisingly instantaneous and intriguingly slow. It unfolded in the way it does when our reality lies outside our expectations. Unfolded, as it always does, to Newton's physical laws of the universe:

1. An object continues to move at a constant velocity unless acted upon by an external force.

2. Force equals mass times acceleration.

3. When one body exerts a force on a second body, the second body simultaneously exerts a force equal in magnitude and opposite in direction on the first body.

My knowledge of high school physics instantly became a brilliant technicolor explosion of blinding white lights, chrome grills, green and orange fenders. The split-second crescendo of grinding, scraping, and crunching steel was followed by a soft hiss and the sweet smell of steaming antifreeze. The right side of my rib cage felt as though I'd been broadsided by the cracking impact of a towering homerun swing.

We had run head on into a slow-moving pickup truck. The impact bounced us back a good ten feet. The safety belt saved my life because it prevented me from catapulting out the front window. I ended up with five broken ribs.

Though unknown to me at the time, this was perhaps the single most transformational moment in my life. So far, anyway.

There are many transformational moments scattered throughout our lives. Each such moment corrects the course of our journey. Some are grand. Some are small. Most events in our life, whether momentous or minuscule, rarely garner our attention for very long, much less create transformation.

What defines a moment as transformational is not its scale or impact as traditionally conceived.

Instead, a transformational moment is a synchronistic event we allow to be meaningful enough to have an impact on how we define ourselves.

The transformational moment exists in the space between who we are and who we are becoming. Technically, then, *every* moment is a transformational moment. We are always moving from who we are to who we are becoming.

Realistically, a moment's existence does not mean we consciously take advantage of it to transform ourselves. Sometimes it takes a deep, shaking event like a car accident to get our attention.

Sometimes, it is just a matter of paying attention.

Transformation, in the context of human consciousness, requires a paradigm shift. A paradigm basically is how we think things work, and we all have them. A paradigm defines our expectations about how experiences will unfold. A paradigm shift can only occur when we change from one way of thinking about or experiencing something to another way of thinking about or experiencing something.

Although paradigm shifts are possible at any moment or place in our day-to-day lives, three factors are required before a paradigm shift can occur:

1. An agent of change.

2. An engaged awareness that something meaningful occurred.

3. The ability to allow the experience to influence the way we define ourselves.

In the case of my car accident, the agent of change was the car accident.

I have often wondered if my agent of change could have been less traumatic. Whether the universe could have corrected the course of my life journey with a more subtle message. I have concluded no. The amount of force necessary to change both the velocity and trajectory of my life was an exact measure of the dose needed to create the paradigm shift that resulted.

Could it have been different?

I have also concluded that the universe identifies our agents of change by performing a continuous symphony of signals for each of us. We ignore most of the signals, treating the symphony like elevator music. Even if we discern a tune, the notes pass by or through us unrecognized and unheeded. I have further concluded that the universe's symphony grows louder — increasingly impossible to categorize as background noise — until we hear it. And it becomes louder still until we listen intently and consciously. Then, louder and more deliberate until we respond intently and consciously.

A transformational moment takes both an agent of change *and* the awareness that something meaningful has transpired.

My moment of awareness occurred as I was leaving the hospital. After a physical exam and x-rays to visualize my broken ribs, the emergency room doctor commented how lucky I was. My paradigm shift began to unfold when I asked the ER doctor what I could do to get better. He looked at me quizzically. He told me to take the pain medication and go home.

His response to my question became the fabled fork in the road that allowed me to shift my group of ideas about how something should be done, made, or thought about.

The medical model my ER doctor followed was to stop disease and repair trauma. I also held that to be true. And why wouldn't I? It's certainly an effective model.

But it left out a critical aspect of human health. In addition to stopping disease and repairing trauma, what else can we — medical professionals and patients alike — do to promote healing of the body? Doesn't healing encompass mental and emotional aspects of our human existence as well as simply our physical bodies?

I was 21 years old. I was sore and achy, wrapped through my torso like a mummy.

I was, indeed, lucky.

I walked out of the warm hospital into the spitting wet snow of that December morning. I looked at the grey sky and thought, "There must be something I can do to help myself heal…."

I walked home, deeply engaged with the sound of my feet on the wet pavement. Deeply engaged with the cold air against the back of my throat. Deeply engaged with the pressure of my beating heart.

I was ready to embark on the third essential factor of transformation. I was ready to allow myself to be affected by this experience. Could diet affect my healing? How about herbs or other supplements? Visualization? Meditation? Live foods?

I began to study and incorporate all these concepts. I took a few classes and eventually found my way to Bastyr University in Seattle. In time, I earned a master's degree in acupuncture and a doctorate in naturopathic medicine.

Daily life presents us with countless agents of change. Every breath offers us the opportunity to experience life differently than the previous breath. However, living a mindful life does not mean we are actively engaged every second of every day in the pursuit of this transformational process.

Living a mindful life means that we are aware of the opportunity that each breath can be more enlightened than the previous breath.

Living a mindful life does not imply that if we are not actively engaged, we are not enlightened. Enlightenment is being able to choose how we define ourselves from moment to moment.

Observing agents of change, and allowing them to be meaningful, moves us into the territory of the transformational moment.

Allowing that moment to effect us is transformational.

Mundane Agents of Change

Aside from an obvious trauma, what else can be an agent of change?

It can seem challenging to create a paradigm shift in our day-to-day life, especially when it seems so patterned. We are creatures of habit. We do the same things in the same ways. How does a paradigm shift occur when it seems as though there is no agent of change?

Practice:

Drive the same street you have driven a thousand times before. As you drive, imagine you are seeing it for the first time. Imagine you are in a foreign country and that you have never gone this way before.

How does that transform your experience?

In this case, our visualization has become the agent of change. We consciously enter that space between the way something has been experienced and the way it can be experienced. Thus, the transformational moment.

The terrain does not change. Only our experience of it changes.

"The real voyage of discovery consists not in seeking new lands but seeing with new eyes."

—Marcel Proust

Let's say you work with someone who irritates you. Say, for example, his behavior is demeaning or hurtful. Your behavior system for dealing with him is to disregard or ignore him. At times, you placate him with a mask of friendliness.

One day you are interacting with him and for just a moment, instead of seeing him as a big oaf and a bully, you visualize him as a little kid. You see him before layers of defensive behavior gelled into place. You see him as a wounded or scared young child.

At that moment, you begin to relax. Your heart softens. Your expanded view of him becomes the agent of change. You allow that few seconds to be meaningful.

This becomes a transformational moment.

You stand in front of the mirror. It's been a long day, perhaps not your best day. You feel beat up by life. You're tired. You're full of unkind thoughts. But somehow you think, "All I have is now. All I can do is love."

This is the making of a transformational moment because that thought can be an agent of change. That thought can instigate a paradigm shift. That thought can move you from one way of thinking or experiencing this day to another way of thinking or experiencing this day.

The question is, do you allow this moment to be meaningful?

Practice:

Honoring Your Life as a Transformational Journey

This is a practice of gratitude for who we are, not what we have or what we do.

Give yourself some time, perhaps an hour or more. Find a place that fosters contemplation, a place free of distractions. Have your journal at hand, and something to write with.

Settle in. Relax your throat, your neck, and your shoulders. Inhale deeply. Exhale any tension or worries.

Do this three times. Each time you exhale, you release tension or worries.

Through deep relaxed breathing, allow your mind to calm. Allow your mind to synchronize with the large, slow, ocean-like swells of the contemplative and meditative states.

A Vision

Now imagine you have come upon a sacred site. It could be a sanctuary of stone or a refuge in nature. Visualize the scene before you. Imagine the details: the sights, sounds, and scents. Imagine how your surroundings feel. Immerse yourself in the texture of the setting.

In this sacred site, you will review your life. You will begin to honor who you are.

As is customary with entering any sacred site, a ritual of purification or sacrifice must be made. Before you can enter this sacred site, you must take off your backpack of self-criticism. You must leave it behind. You must remove and abandon all the jagged words and cutting thoughts, all the piercing judgments, the thousand voices of self-deprecation.

Visualize striding into the sacred site you created with no burdens.

Move deeper into the site. Find a place to settle in. This is where you will sit in contemplation.

Begin to visualize the transformational moments in your life. Visualize the moments you allowed to be meaningful enough to transform your sense of self through your strength and insight.

As you do this, envision this conversation with the universe:

ME: Yes, I see those moments when I walked with integrity. Yes, I see those moments when my heart was pure. Yes, I see those moments when I stood with honor in the face of fear. I can acknowledge those times. Yet, as I review my life, I also see those moments when I struggled. I see those moments when I didn't stand up, step forward, or name the truth. I see those moments when I hid or was too scared or embarrassed to express myself. Yes, I see those moments when I hurt and when I failed.

UNIVERSE: Yes, these were just practice opportunities. Yes, you have practiced hundreds — maybe thousands — of them in your lifetime. Opportunity. Stumble. Opportunity. Fail. Opportunity. Hurt, pain, or loss. Practice and practice again. Learn what you do not know. That is the nature of the evolution of the soul. You will need many opportunities to practice before you can resolve and transform behaviors you have carried through lifetimes. You have traveled far. Your journey took great courage to cross the span of lifetimes and arrive here, now, seated at this sacred site. I honor you. I see how courageous you are.

From this contemplative state, honor your life as a journey. With kindness and patience note some of the transformational moments in your life. Record them in your journal.

9

Energy Follows Consciousness

Where attention goes, energy flows;
Where intention goes, energy flows.

—James Redfield

ENERGY FOLLOWS CONSCIOUSNESS and manifests into the physical world.

It would be safe to say that you are not thinking about your feet. Until now. Your consciousness has moved towards the floor, or the foot of the bed or couch or wherever your feet may be.

Have you ever gotten cold feet? This idiom is true. It refers to feeling scared. When we are scared, our energy moves up and out of our body. When we are startled, we pull up and back.

This is an exercise that will demonstrate that energy follows consciousness and then manifests into the physical world.

This exercise can be done with either two or three people.

Two people

The person you work with must be willing to let you lift them off the floor. The best way to do this is to hold them in a bear hug from behind. Think about performing the Heimlich maneuver. The person you will lift can have their arms at their side or crossed over their chest like a mummy.

It is important to do this exercise respectfully and with permission. It works great with children.

Ask the person you will pick up to think of something that weighs very little, such as a balloon, butterflies, or a feather. Now gently lift them off the floor. It doesn't need to be high. A few inches is enough. And then set them down.

Now ask the person to think of something heavy, such as a rock, or to imagine they are glued to the ground. Now, just as you did when you asked the person to think of something light, gently lift them.

You will discover that this person, who's weight has not changed in moments between thinking of something light and something heavy, is difficult — if not impossible — to lift.

Interesting, isn't it?

Three people

In this version of the exercise, two people lift one person off the floor.

The person being lifted starts with their arms at their side and then bends their arms 90 degrees at the elbows, as though carrying a tray.

The two people lifting gently but firmly hold the elbow and the wrist on the same side of the person being lifted.

The person being lifted keeps their elbows in and shoulders strong as the arms become the leverage point to lift the body.

Have the person you will pick up think of something light. Now gently lift them and return them to the floor.

Now have the person think of something heavy or of being glued to the ground. Gently lift and return them.

As in the two-person exercise, the lifting partners will discover that the person becomes harder to lift even though their weight hasn't changed.

How is this possible? The only variable is our conscious thought. We become heavier or lighter because our energy, through intention, has responded to our conscious thought. Our energy has become manifest in the physical world.

10

Taking Inventory, also known as Breathe - Ground - Relax

[W]hether it's awareness of the body, awareness of the mind, awareness of your emotions, awareness of your relationships, or awareness of your environment.
I think the key to transforming your life is to be aware of who you are.

—Deepak Chopra

AWARENESS IS KEY to transformation and is an essential first step in self-discovery.

Awareness allows us to take an objective inventory of both who and how we are in the world. As we expand our awareness, we broaden our sense of self and deepen our sense of empowerment.

One of the ways we expand our awareness is to enter the mindful practice of taking inventory. This chapter introduces the practice of taking inventory, which we will see empowers us to respond — instead of merely react — to events and people in our life.

Let's begin by defining what it means to react or be reactive.

If at any point, in any situation, at any time, you feel tense, your breath shortens, or if you lose your sense of self, you are in a *reaction*.

A reactive state, or reaction, occurs when we feel threatened. When we are in a reaction, our bodies respond physiologically, and we become ungrounded.

A threat, or fearing a threat, signals the amygdala (a small almond shaped organ in the center of our brain) to activate our autonomic nervous system (ANS). Stimulating the ANS has physiological effects: heart rate increases, blood pressure goes up, breathing quickens, muscles tighten, and stress hormones flood our bodies. This is the classic fight, flight, or freeze reaction.

No matter how mindful, advanced, spiritual, or evolved you may be, as we further explore this topic you likely will be surprised just how often you find yourself in a reaction.

The goal in living mindfully is to notice how often we are reacting and to make a choice to consciously move from this reactive state to a response.

A response, in contrast to a reaction, is when our physiology demonstrates that we are fully present, free of tension in our physical body, relaxed in our breath, and deeply grounded in our energy. There is a balance between our mental process, our emotional world, and our physical body.

In a responsive state, our cellular system is not in a fight, flight, or freeze mode. We do not don the "I'm OK" mask as our body tenses and our breathing stops. Our behavior is true to who we are in the present authentic moment.

The scholar Joseph Campbell states it well: "The goal of life is to make your heartbeat match the beat of the universe, to match your nature with Nature."

In our mindful efforts to explore who we are and to deepen relational contact, it is vitally important for us to distinguish a reaction from a response because when we are in a reaction, we simply are not in contact.

We can use our physical body as an instrument to help us figure out when we are in a reaction and when we are in a response. As we do this, we bring greater awareness to the who and how we are at any moment. From there, we can consciously take the steps necessary to become present and to deepen our relational contact. This is exceptionally useful and very empowering.

To add some perspective, it is valuable to know that our reactionary behavior is driven by our subconscious mind, triggered by a pattern that has been hardwired into our circuitry since early childhood. This is a limbic system reaction. It happens in microseconds. It completely bypasses our higher functioning frontal lobe's task of rational thought.

Because we are wired to automatically fight, flee, or freeze, moving from a reaction to a response can be challenging. Fortunately, despite the challenge, it is not particularly complicated.

The challenge exists because we are so frequently prompted into a reaction by something in our environment: a person, a situation, a dynamic at home or at work, just about anything. Subconsciously, a reactive pattern or behavior effects our body on physical, mental, and emotional levels.

We react because our subconscious believes we are unsafe or threatened in some way. For the most part, this makes no rational sense. A good example of this is gathering with family over the Thanksgiving holiday. Ever feel tense in situations like this?

Taking inventory of our physical, mental, and emotional levels reveals whether we are in a reaction or a response. Taking inventory empowers us to move from a reaction to a response.

Physical

The sounds were alive and foreign to my ears. The mesmerizing call of the laughing falcon: *gua-co... gua-co... gua-co.* The buzz and twirl of a thousand insects. The eerie wail of the howler monkey. The air was saturated and dense and oh so soft.

I know exactly when it happened. It was the third day of our trip. As I walked back from the market, I realized that my body felt strange. It felt different. My shoulders had dropped. My legs felt warm. My breath was deep and easy. What did these strange sensations mean?

If you are like me, you probably carry some tension in your physical body. I never thought I was particularly tense until I took a much-needed vacation in the tropical forests of Costa Rica.

For most of us, a fair degree of muscle tension is our normal baseline. It's so normal that we don't fully recognize just how tense we really are.

Practice:

To use the physical body as an instrument and to take inventory, we first have to connect to it.

Here is a two-part exercise to discover our baseline of tension and to help us connect to our physical body.

Part One: Make yourself comfortable, sitting or lying. Give your body a gentle shake through your shoulders, torso, hips, and legs. Take a breath and gently relax into an exhale. Repeat this a couple of times.

Now add tension to your body. Squeeze your buttocks, belly, chest, and shoulders. Hold your body tight for the count of five, and then let go. Let your shoulders drop, your abdomen soften, and your back relax.

Do this three times.

You can expand this exercise to include your legs, feet, hands, any part of the body — even your eyes!

By doing this exercise a couple of times over a few days, you will begin to tune into your body and its baseline tension. This exercise will also help you release the chronic tension that is so familiar you might have thought it was normal.

The more you tune your instrument in this way, the more you will enhance your mind-body connection. This is an essential aspect in improving our ability to take inventory.

Part Two: Initially, it will be useful to stage this exercise. After a bit of practice, you will be able to confidently use this tool in the real world of relationships.

It is important to start with Part One of this practice. As you complete Part One, allow yourself to end in a relaxed state.

Only after you are at a relaxed baseline can Part Two begin.

Part Two, Step 1: From your relaxed baseline, contemplate a stressful aspect of your life. Perhaps it's at work or a problem with your neighbor. Family is always rich fodder for stressors. The topic you focus on doesn't really matter. What matters is that you bring your awareness to the mind-body connection. What matters is that you find the part of your body that tightens when you think about this stressful aspect of your life.

Don't worry that you won't be able to find it. After you contemplate a stressor, some part of your physical body will be more tense than it was at your relaxed state.

By definition, you are in a reaction. On some level, you feel threatened — even if it is only by contemplating a stressful aspect of your life. Your body has gone into a fight, flight, or freeze reaction. Remember, if you are tense or your breathing is short, you are in a reaction.

Part Two, Step 2: As best you can, relax your body. Contemplate anything not stressful: the beach, birds, a flowing river.

Part Two, Step 3: Repeat this exercise a couple of times. Start in a relaxed state. Contemplate a stressful situation. Notice where you get tense. End in that place where you are tense from contemplating a stressful situation in your life.

Part Two, Step 4: At that moment — at that place of tension — you are at the threshold of a transformational moment. With consciousness, you are able to make a choice: do you react, or do you respond?

This choice is the hallmark of enlightenment.

The transformational gem occurs when you contemplate this stressful situation and consciously relax the part of your body that is tense. This sends a signal to your mind-body connection. It moves you out of fight, flight, or freeze.

You choose to give your cellular system a different experience. You break a pattern, a habit, a reaction driven by your belief system.

Your choice allows you to come out of reaction.

The gift of this practice is that you begin to use your body as an instrument.

First, by tuning into your baseline tension.

Second, by consciously moving from tension to relaxation when confronted by a stressor.

Not surprisingly, by paying a bit of attention you will notice that your day-to-day life gives you dozens of opportunities to witness and practice this dynamic of mindfully moving from tension to relaxation.

Practice:

Now we get to take our practice sessions into the world of relationships.

With awareness, you will notice that when out and about in your daily life, some part of your body — perhaps your neck, shoulders, or legs — has tightened. Almost always, this tension is triggered when we are in real-time, face-to-face relationships with other people. Of course, this does not always happen, but if you note the subtle body tensions that occur as you interact with others, you will be surprised how often it does.

Once you have identified the tension in your body, begin to consciously relax it. This is the same practice you undertook in your mind and body during the two-part exercise.

Don't worry if you find this challenging at first. It is challenging. Remember — we are reprogramming deeply held cellular patterns.

Let's not forget our breath.

When we are tense, we are not breathing. The paradigm of tension in the body we just explored holds true for our breathing pattern. In your daily life, as you find yourself relating to someone else or facing a stressful dynamic or thought, simply notice your breath:

Are you breathing at all?

How?

Is it relaxed or shallow?

This, in addition to noticing your level of tension, is another way to use your body as an instrument to take inventory.

Once you have witnessed your breathing (it will almost always be restricted), consciously inhale gently and exhale in a relaxed sigh. Breathe into your belly. Again, this signals your body-mind connection to come out of a reaction.

These two simple actions — relaxing tension and breathing deeply — will always move you from reactive state to a responsive state.

Do not underestimate the power of these two simple actions because they are simple. They are among the most empowering actions we can take. Consciously relaxing and breathing deeply essentially reprograms our habitual pattern of living in a reactive state. These two simple actions offer us the cellular experience of living in a responsive state.

Grounding

Breathing and relaxing sets the stage for grounding.

Grounding is an essential component of coming fully present into our physical body.

Remember that energy follows consciousness. Bring your awareness to your feet, to the floor and the ground below you. Bring your consciousness to the center of the earth. Grounding is about bringing our awareness and our energy through our physical body to connect into the earth. By grounding, we come out of our heads. There is a sinking feeling, a relaxing of the hips and legs, a heaviness that feels as though we are magnetically connected to the ground. It can kinesthetically mimic the dropping sensation one gets when riding down in an elevator.

By grounding, we open the first chakra. We feel safe and solid in the physical world. With grounding, breathing, and relaxing we are able to move our autonomic nervous system out of the flight, fight, freeze (reaction) and into our parasympathetic system of rest/ relax/ recover (response).

As long as we are human, we will have reactions. We will demand that others be different. We will get upset when they are not. We will perceive deadly threats even when, objectively, the threats don't truly ascend to a life-or-death matter.

The goal of mindful living and transformational work is to shorten the time we devote to our reaction. Some reactions last a lifetime in the form of a habit. If we could decrease that reaction to only a few days, imagine the resources we could free from needless worry and dedicate to more useful, productive pursuits. And if we can shorten a reactive state from a lifetime to a few days, why not shorten it to a couple hours?

The grandest of all mindful interventions is to respond in a single moment — to make a conscious choice that allows us to witness our reactive behavior and at the same time transform it to a response.

Now that we've addressed the physical level of moving from a reaction to a response, let's do the same with mental and emotional levels.

Mental

A reaction occurs when we perceive (either objectively or not) a threat. The very nature of a reaction bypasses the cognitive thought process because fight, flight, or freeze is not a left-brain, rational process. It is governed by our nervous system and hormonal process. A reaction is geared to survival and was designed over eons of objectively very threatening lifetimes. When our body-mind system registers a threat, our physiology — down to the cellular level — reacts even before our higher executive-function brain knows what's going on.

We know that about 90% of our behavior is driven by the sub-conscious aspect of our psyche. Only about 10% of how we interact with our world is driven by rational thought. Yet this 10% of our mental being offers us two very valuable gifts:

Observation and choice.

To explore the mental aspect of this taking-inventory paradigm, we need to use these two profound gifts together.

Observation, or becoming the witness, is one of the most powerful roles we can take in our Great Quest to live a mindful life.

As we are able to move into the witness role (with practice) we are able to objectively survey the ongoing drama of our current situation. From this place of the nonattached observer, we can begin to take inventory of ourselves and who and how we are in any situation.

Living Life in a Reaction

On many fronts, my first marriage was filled with strife. Our communication was rooted in argument and blame. Often, it devolved into the nonverbal gruffness that comes from being upset or angry and behaving in that time-tested pattern of withdrawing or withholding. This was our norm. Discord could last for hours or days.

We did not dedicate ourselves to our marriage or resolving unhealthy patterns. Instead, each of us was dedicated to being right.

We squandered our time naively hoping or expecting that we could get the other to change or demanding that the other become a different person.

Of course, with clear vision, we know today any hope or expectation that the other will change or be different is futile. Yet, somehow, we remain undeterred as we harbor the desire that our hopes and expectations will someday, in some way, bear fruit.

The reason we harbor this elusive goal is simple. We believe that if the other changes, our lives will be easier.

Personal transformation and living a life that supports the evolution of our soul's journey can be downright hard at times. If the people around us would only change, be different, or act accordingly, we would have less strife in our lives.

Or so we falsely believe.

On a few fronts, my first marriage was very successful. We had an amazing daughter and raised our family through the lean years of medical school. Looking back, there is plenty of blame to go around. But today, with the gift of hindsight, insight, and personal work, I can say that it wasn't the marriage that was unsuccessful.

It was me who was unsuccessful.

I was unsuccessful moving from a reactive state to a responsive state. In fact, I didn't even know there was such an option at that point. I spent hours — even days — in a reaction. Thinking that the other was to blame, I shut down, withheld my love, ignored any potential connection, and grunted my communication.

Living Life in a Response

Young children currently live in our home. It is common for me to arrive after a full day's work and find the house in a high level of disarray. There are coats piled in the closet, backpacks in front of the door, and an explosion of socks on the floor, table, and couch. The youngest of the children wants to jump into my arms and share her artwork.

Suffice to say, I relax more easily in a neat and orderly environment. Walking into this situation creates tension in my body and an upwelling urge to yell, "Pick up your stuff!"

That is a reaction. This is my response.

I take inventory:

I notice the tension in my body. I notice my breathing is tight. I notice I am uncomfortable. I feel anger and frustration about the mess. I think, "Here's what needs to be done to fix this situation."

I observe:

I observe my habitual impulse to tell others what to do so I can be relaxed.

I choose:

I slow my mind. I take a breath. I relax my shoulders. I grab the youngest, clear a spot on the couch, and listen with full presence to her day's adventure. This feels good, heartfelt, kind.

This is a response.

This mundane event — coming home from work — becomes a transformational moment because the action I chose is not driven by habit.

Now that we've addressed the physical and mental levels of moving from a reaction to a response, let's do the same with the emotional level.

Emotional

Our emotions can be overwhelming. They can be exhilarating, as when we fall in love. They can be exhausting, as when we go through a divorce.

Our emotional body is very sensitive and highly tuned to the influences in our environment. We have all had "this doesn't feel right" experiences.

In taking inventory, emotions play a critical role. They can be like the canary in the coal mine, transmitting information that is too subtle for our physical or mental process.

"How do I feel?"

That's the most valuable question.

It may be as simple a question as, "Do I feel good, happy, safe? Or do I feel scared, anxious, threatened?"

It is not necessary to know *why* you might feel a certain way. However, it is imperative to know that you do feel something. There is power in recognizing and witnessing how you feel. It allows you to further discover how that feeling affects your physical body and your thought process.

Emotions that affect the physical body are the sensations we feel on a cellular level. If we feel scared, our physical sensation might be tension or shallow breathing, or both. If we feel anger, our physical sensation might be pressure and a pounding heart.

Curiosity about our feelings can bring awareness of our physical sensations. This enhances the mind-body connection. It allows us to use the body as an instrument to take inventory.

Curiosity and awareness do not necessarily resolve our habitual body tension. They do not cause to vanish the habit of guarding ourselves or the belief system that the world is not safe. They do not explain why we often feel anxious, scared, or threatened for no discernible reason.

But they do, in real-time, allow us to respond to the moment instead of merely reacting to our world. They allow us to create a sense of safety and presence in our own body and psyche.

The Takeaway

By attending to our own internal world, we can create an experience of safety and presence. From that place, we are able to deeply attend to and make contact with the external world and fellow human beings with whom we share our lives.

Understanding the physical, mental, and emotional levels of reactions and responses is surprisingly simple and profoundly effective. It empowers us to take inventory of our mind-body connection and to become aware of how we are interfacing with our environment.

It enables us to consciously, mindfully choose to move from a reaction to a response.

11

Consciousness Travels an Evolutionary Arc

One does not become enlightened by imagining figures of light,
but by making the darkness conscious.
The latter procedure, however, is disagreeable
and therefore not popular.

—C.G. Jung

OUR CONSCIOUSNESS TRAVELS an evolutionary arc as we integrate our life experiences and broaden our awareness. This evolution occurs over four phases.

Phase 1: We are aware something is happening, but we don't know what it is.

In this phase, it's common to be confused or frustrated by, or even oblivious to, what is objectively going on around us. We are unable to see the causal connection between our actions and how the world reacts to our actions. We either don't "get it" or we spend time blaming others for our experiences. We spend a lot of time muttering "Huh!" or "What?"

Phase 2: We are aware something happened after it happens.

This is the classic insight or understanding that comes hours or days after an incident. In this phase, we need time and space to expand our awareness and process our experiences. With distance from an experience, something clicks in the space that time creates, and we see a greater dynamic at play. Instead of muttering "Huh!", we exclaim, "Oh, now I get it!"

Phase 3: We are aware of what is happening as it happens.

This phase is a hallmark of broadened awareness. We are solidly in the witness role. We can observe ourselves and the dynamics around us without judgement.

Or, we can observe that we:

- Do have judgment.
- Are not observing.
- Are angry, sad, or blaming the other.
- Really care and are trying.
- Really don't care but are pretending we do to get what we want.

The hallmark of this phase is that we are able to observe objectively what is happening both within and without us.

We get to see the relationship patterns driven by our belief systems. We can observe the familiar, habitual behaviors driven by our subconscious. We can see the impact patterns and habits have on our relationships. In this phase, in the unfolding moment, we might subtly murmur "Hmm" or "A-ha" to ourselves.

Phase 4: We are aware that something is happening in the present moment and we are able to choose in that moment to move from reaction to response.

Once we've achieved the mindfulness of Phase 4, we embody the higher attributes of the mental level of taking inventory: observation and choice. We become empowered. Arguably, this is one of the most empowered places we can be. We say to ourselves, "Oh, now I get it… and here's what I can do about it."

This becomes our transformational moment. As in all transformational moments, we get to make a choice instead of simply manifesting a habit. We can choose to move from a reaction to a response. We are in a state of being that is devoid of blame and demands.

A relaxed sigh of patience, gratitude, and presence is infused into our breath, and we are able to embody a heartfelt connection.

PART FOUR

True Needs

The Gift of Being Wrong

There is nothing noble in being superior to your fellow man;
true nobility is being superior to your former self.

—Ernest Hemingway

To be wrong is one of the most profound and liberating experiences that a mindful life will offer.

It can also be one of the most challenging.

In our Great Quest for mindfulness and transformation, being wrong goes beyond apologizing for our slights and trespasses. Being wrong embraces humility. It requires a great dose of courage. Beyond the habitual "I'm sorry," being wrong also says:

- I am willing to be wrong so I can be whole.

- I am willing to set aside the belief systems that drive my dedication to how I believe life and I are — or should be.

- I am willing to set aside the belief systems that drive my dedication to how I believe others and life should be.

- I am willing to set aside the patterned demands I put on myself and others.

Being wrong liberates us:

- I relinquish my attachment to being right or self-righteous.

- I relinquish my attachment to feeling hurt.

- I relinquish my attachment to being a victim.

Being wrong is a state of acceptance:

- I accept that I will become undefended.

- I accept that I must listen to the truth of what is being said and not being said.

- I accept other points of view without bias.

- I accept my neutral, open-hearted role as witness.

In other words, being wrong means that you are able to respond — not merely react — to the present moment.

She was in her mid-30's, this patient of mine. Her world was chaotic and exhausting. Storm after storm of personal trauma had flattened her faith, stunted her stamina, and extinguished her sense of self. Hoping to keep the storm at bay, she'd shuttered her windows and withdrawn from the world.

Unfortunately, that only deepened a sense of isolation. It did little to dampen the howling winds that rattled her soul.

The sense of isolation always involves the heart, for it is through the heart that we make our relational connections. It's common and even understandable that, due to the sensitive nature of our hearts, our initial reaction to loss and trauma is to isolate and insulate this most sensitive of all our feeling centers.

The current squall in her life had to do with her brother. Her brother was the wayward one of their family. He was always plotting the next big score, the one that would turn his life around. He was estranged from his wife. He was filled with hate for his father. He blamed the world for his plight.

My client bore the brunt of his anger and blame. Far too many times, she'd had to place her heart behind an iron shield. Protection, she said, from her brother's harsh onslaught.

My client believed that her angst and pain would resolve if only her brother started loving himself. If only her brother would be responsible for his actions instead of blaming everyone else.

She knew she was right about this. If only her brother were different, she would be less distraught.

Just as important, and just as unspoken, she wanted to feel loved. She wanted her brother to see her. She wanted her brother to accept her and the efforts she put forth. This dynamic was deeply painful.

And, true to human nature, she put the blame for her pain onto another person.

I asked her if she could stop blaming her brother for failing to love her as she felt he should.

"I've tried," she responded. "I'm working on it. But he is too self-righteous, and I've been hurt too many times. He needs to open up."

To experience transformation, live more mindfully, and get unstuck, I invited my client to enter the territory of being wrong. As she courageously entered this terrain, she began to discover her demand that her brother be different was the nexus of her pain. From this point we began to explore how her demand could not be met — but her true need for connection and love could be.

True Needs Reflect our Deepest Longings

Driving our demands is a longing for a true need to be satisfied.

Let's say we long for acceptance. It could be any longing —
for love or a partner, for health or fitness, for a family or sense of
belonging, for a career or money. Every one of us, in accord with
our unique incarnational contracts, has some aspect of our life that
eludes our ability to manifest. This elusive aspect — love, health,
or money — becomes the territory where our most consequential
life experiences play out.

An incarnational contract is the accord our soul co-creates with
the universe prior to incarnation. In this accord are the probable
topics and territories of life experience deemed most consequential
for our evolutionary development.

The incarnational contract is created in the same fashion as
a guidance counselor would share a review of our strengths and
weaknesses with a teacher. The teacher (or, in the case of our incarnational contracts, the universe) can then best support our growth
with experiences and lessons tailored to our evolutionary needs.
Would the territories of acceptance, rejection, and judgment offer
the most profound evolutionary experiences in this life? Would
those experiences — if we met them with awareness, kindness, and
insight — allow us to up our game and graduate into the next level
of enlightenment?

The goal, of course, is to use these sacredly tailored life experiences to develop aspects of ourselves that are ripe for maturation.

The goal is to manifest what has been elusive.

And in doing so, we develop and broaden aspects of ourselves
that further the evolution of our soul.

Aspects and Territories for Evolution

How do you know on what trail our most consequential evolutionary journey travels?

You will be intimately familiar with your most consequential territory because it is what you have yet to manifest in your life. It is what you long for. It is what you struggle with.

It is your Great Quest.

Practice:

When you've got some time, find a quiet place and start by completing this sentence:

What I long for, what I struggle with, and what I have yet to manifest is _____.

Some common quests we encounter include:

Self-worth	Health	Career
Communication	Intimacy and Trust	Goals
Family	Finances	Spirituality
Creativity	Education	Love

After you have identified your longing, respond to this question:

How am I not expressing what I long for?

In the example of longing for acceptance, we know that self-acceptance and acceptance of others is an evolutionary aspect of our developing consciousness. Therefore, we know that we will walk through the rough and tangled terrain of rejection. Only through the painful experience of rejection can we practice acceptance.

This paradox is the same for any territory. If I long for health, it is because I experience illness. If I long for love, it is because I experience heartache.

Fortunately, the mindful question to ask is always the same even if the territory changes. Apply your Great Quest to respond to — or develop for yourself and then respond to — the relevant mindful paradox in your journal:

If I long for acceptance, how do I judge and reject myself and others?

If I long for love, how do I fail to love myself and others?

If I long for money, how am I poor — literally or metaphorically?

If I long for health, how am I not healthy — in thought or deed?

After you have identified your longing and explored your answer to the mindful paradox, identify and journal opportunities to make progress on your Great Quest:

These are opportunities for me to fulfill my longing. How can I be more accepting, loving, wealthy, healthy, or _____ in my:

- Thoughts
- Feelings
- Actions

This practice is more than accepting oneself or loving oneself.

This is the path that — when mindfully traveled — leads us towards holding and being that which we long to receive.

In this example of *acceptance,* we will demand that the other accept us. When the other doesn't, we blame the other for not accepting us. This blame leaves us longing for acceptance. We get tense. We feel anguish. We feel rejected.

Now imagine I demand that you accept me. I get tense and blame you when you don't respond to my demand. Does this foster a relationship in which you would want to accept me? Does that foster a relationship in which I experience acceptance?

Not likely. And our behavior becomes a self-fulfilling cycle.

Until we resolve our own inability to accept ourselves and others, we will never feel accepted.

My client came to see me because she was stuck. By all accounts, she was overwhelmed and under-supported. She couldn't see forward through the gale and the mist and the fog of the storms. Yet, like a windblown leaf, she had landed in my office. She found herself not lost, but at a crossroads.

To experience transformation and move forward — to get unstuck — she had to be wrong. We began to explore how the demand that her brother be different could not be met — but her true need for connection and love could be.

In transformational work, being wrong allows us to become whole. It allows us to enter the territory of truly being happy, holy, wealthy, and healthy.

My patient began to discover that the demand she put on her brother was really an opportunity to create the experience of what she longed for within herself.

Our True Task

The transformational endeavor here was for her to acknowledge she was wrong about what her task was. She had to set aside the demand that her brother be any different, because that was not her task. Her task was to open her heart to him and accept him wherever he is in his life. This acceptance is not the same as agreeing with him. It is not the same as colluding with him. It is not creating codependent behavior.

The critical insight here is that setting aside demands has nothing to do with others.

It has everything to do with what is alive within us.

Not having a demand is more pleasurable and certainly healthier than holding a demand. The same is true for opening the heart. It is not about the other. It is about the pleasure we feel in our body as we let energy and love move through our heart.

It is simply the most powerful place we can be when in relationship with another: present, accepting, open-hearted.

The Embodiment of Our Longing

At that crossroads in my office, my courageous patient was able to admit she was wrong about her task. A shift occurred. She accepted the right task. The iron shield began to dissolve. She felt love flow through her heart.

She held that which she wanted to experience. She felt connected to her difficult, distant, wayward brother.

Her demand diminished. The demand that he do or be a particular thing faded. Her true need became fulfilled. Her true need — feeling a heart connection — occurred. From that point, she chose to walk in a new direction. She chose to walk away from the bitterness, withholding, sniping, and frustration of demands. She chose to walk towards the wholeness of meeting her need for a heart connection.

She held in her system the exact experience she wanted to receive. She created the experience. She experienced the experience, and she became the experience — the experience of an open-hearted connection. Thus, her true need was met.

The Takeaway

We are not here to demand of others. We are here to see that our own true needs are met. That is the mindful life. Our behavior and the kind of person we are have nothing to do with what someone else says or does. No one can prevent you from loving. No one can prevent you from being accepting. It takes less energy to love than to hate, though it can feel riskier.

The solution may be challenging, but it is not complicated.

We give to the other that which we long to receive. We become that which we long to receive. In doing so, we experience what it is we long for. This broadens the way we have always identified ourselves. And now we get to share this expanded sense of self with others.

What a gracious gift.

13

Needs versus Demands

Immature love says, "I love you because I need you."
Mature love says, "I need you because I love you."

—Erich Fromm

WHEN WE WANT, expect, or long for something, how do we know if it is a true need or just a demand? Is there a difference between true needs and demands and what is the difference?

This chapter explores this and the following truth:

The fewer demands I have, the happier I become.

I stood barefoot in the cool damp grass. The bees, humming their songs of love and devotion, hovered over purple clover. The summer sun warmed my face and stirred the sweet morning air. Butterflies lined the railing, drying their wings in the day's first light. The chickens, strutting as chickens do, bustled and crackled like first arrivals at the Saturday flea market.

We had planned to go somewhere that delightful summer morning, though I can't remember where. Since breakfast we had been gathering whatever items were needed for our adventure. Water and hats and sunscreen were likely items for the list. With grandkids and dogs running around, our 9:00 AM deadline had come and gone.

My relaxed state was giving way to tension.

We had agreed to 9:00 AM — how hard was that? It's just a matter of getting in the car and going.

When I have a demand, I insist that something particular be fulfilled to make me whole or happy. I demand someone do something to alleviate the angst I am experiencing.

Demands are driven by the insistence that "only if" someone or some facet of life — or even some aspect of myself — were different, things would be easier or better.

Or so I believed.

I believed because I had not yet come to understand the real issue. It's another paradox. If the impulse that drives my demands is supposed to make life easier and better by having my demands met, why am I happier when I have fewer demands?

The Effects of Demands on Our Physical Body

Practice:

Find your journal and something to write with. Take a few moments and center yourself.

Relax your belly. Breathe gently into your lower abdomen. Loosen your shoulders.

Allow your mind to slow. You might even daydream.

Listen to the sounds around you.

Bring yourself to the present moment, free of past or future distractions.

Breathe slowly into that relaxed belly. Notice how you feel physically and emotionally. Breathe again and release, as best you can, any tension as you exhale.

Now visualize a situation in your life when <u>you demanded</u> that someone do something or be someone they are not. It could have been a spoken or unspoken demand. Some common examples include:

- Pick up after yourself.

- Put the dishes in the sink.

- Get your life together.

- Pay attention to me.

- Be on time.

In your journal, write your demand.

Repeat your demand aloud a few times.

Notice what your body feels like when you project this demand outward. Does it affect your breathing and state of relaxation? Do you feel more tension and angst than before you uttered your demand?

This is not about who picks up the clothes or whether someone listens to you. It is about the sensation you feel in your physical body when you hold a demand.

It is about using this insight and the sensations in your body as a tool to mindfully navigate life.

If you had no demand, would that feel different in your body, your mind, and your emotions?

Answer in your journal. This is how my demand affects me:

- My physical sensations.
- My mental state.
- My emotional condition.

Practice:

Again, take a moment to center yourself by breathing into your lower abdomen.

Loosen your shoulders. Let your thoughts drift away with each gentle exhale.

Listen to the sounds around you. Bring yourself to the present moment, free of distractions.

Take another breath or two into that relaxed belly.

Notice how you feel physically and emotionally. Again, let go of any tension as best you can.

Now, instead of you projecting a demand on someone else, consider what happens when someone else makes a <u>demand on you</u>? Some common spoken and unspoken examples include:

- Pick up your clothes.
- Turn the lights off.
- Get your life together.
- Get a job that pays.
- Fold the laundry.
- Drive the speed limit.
- Care about recycling as much as I do.
- I want you to always know what I want, even if I don't tell you.

In your journal, write the demands that others place on you (or the demands you place on yourself).

Consider how each demand affects your emotions, your breathing, and your level of tension. Use your journal to record your reactions to the demands placed on you.

Demands carry very powerful morphic fields. A morphic field is a constellation of all that is known and has been experienced through time as it pertains to a specific topic. An example of a morphic field is the study and practice of acupuncture.

When I practice acupuncture and place a needle in an acupuncture point, I am doing so with the gravitas of 5,000 years of all the experience, knowledge, feelings, thoughts, and actions that has surrounded this healing modality.

Similarly, with demands, we tap into the accumulated human experience of what it is to insist, control, or command that something be done in a particular way.

The morphic field of a demand has no space for dialogue or open communication.

Consequently, demands evoke strong reactions. These reactions are the sensations we feel in our body. They occur whenever we put a demand on someone, or someone puts a demand on us. If you feel tension, angst, controlled or controlling, you are experiencing the morphic field of demand. If you hold your breath with hope, expectation, or insistence that someone or something be a particular way, you are experiencing the morphic field of demand.

The dog was fed. The dishwasher hummed and churned. Lunch was packed. Most of the crew was in the car. Others were heading that way. With hopes now set on departing before 10:00 AM, I set out to look for my eight-year-old granddaughter, Bella Tejah.

I found her coming through the door with a small basket in her hands. She was excited — smiling and happy. She'd remembered to gather the morning eggs from the chickens. It's her favorite chore.

"Come on," I said. "Get in the car, we have to go."

Except it wasn't my voice I heard. It was my father's.

Time slowed. I saw not the words, but the impact of those words. My words carried a demand. They were steeped in frustration.

My demand stated that if Bella Tejah were in the car, my life would be easier. I would not be tense and frustrated. I would not feel rushed. I would not feel that I needed to control the events of the morning.

In an instant, the slow-motion unfolding of events became a transformational moment. I saw Tejah darken. Her chest collapsed. Her shoulders slumped. Gone was the happy, smiling, excited child.

I love Tejah. I would never do anything to hurt her.

Except I did.

A demand is the insistence, as though by right, that something be a particular way. It could be an external demand that we project out onto our world, as I did with Tejah. It could be one of those familiar internal demands that dogs us daily, nipping at the heels of our innermost thoughts:

- Lose that 20 pounds
- Start exercising
- Do something with your life

A demand creates tension in our body, push in our action, and controlling thoughts in our mind. It creates pain in relationships.

The difference between a True Need and a Demand

There are two critical distinctions between a *true need* and a demand.

First, a *true need* arises from a place of integrated awareness. It arises with an understanding of what is essential to make us materially and spiritually happy, holy, healthy, and wealthy.

In contrast, a demand is an unhealthy, unconsciously developed attempt to control or blame another for what we don't have or can't do.

Second, and this is very important, a *true need* can be met but a demand can never be met. Ever.

Discovering Relationship Demands

We can put demands on ourselves just as easily as we put them on others. Of course, others can and do put their demands on us.

To discover a demand, pick someone in your life who is doing or not doing something you think they should not or should be doing.

We know we've successfully discovered a demand when our physical body grows tense, our breath shortens, and we feel irritated. Insistence permeates us. We make judgments. Our thoughts start and end with "should." Demands, shoulds, and judgments always go together.

Practice:

Write in your journal the names of people you put demands on — including your own. List all your demands under it. Don't edit, second guess, or judge your demands. Here are a few examples:

Share your feelings.

Love me.

Be honest.

Get real.

Know my needs (without me telling you).

Listen to me.

Be less messy.

Do something with your life.

Be patient.

Be present.

Take care of me.

Be mindful.

Talk less.

Be on time.

Grow up.

Don't be so dang needy.

Drive faster.

Look good.

Once you've written your demands, commit to spend time being mindful about them. There are two aspects of demands to be mindful of:

First, witness the frequency of your demands.

Be honest with yourself. Be objective. Use your journal. Almost every time you want something or someone to be different it is a demand. Just notice how often that happens. Be a witness.

And, do your demands have any impact on your body-mind connection? (The answer is yes). How?

Second, witness the impact that your demand has on the other.

The story I shared about Tejah is an example. Pick a time commitment that comfortably fits your schedule. Your commitment might be an hour or a whole day. Notice the impact of your demands on others. How does it affect them? How does it affect your relationship? Journal your observations.

I stood in that slow, unfolding moment of time. The warmth of the sun. The sweet morning air. My granddaughter poised in the doorway.

The manifest world had reflected the impact of my demand. I swear I was possessed by and was channeling my father. That's not an excuse. It was a moment of awakening awareness. It was a startling clear insight into how insidiously our behavior is hardwired into our subconscious by our earliest teachers — our parents.

I vowed, in the earliest of my subconscious childhood, that I would never act like my father. And yet here I was, decades beyond the inception of that vow, behaving just like my father. I had done to my granddaughter what my father had, many times, done to me. He demanded that I be or do things a specific way. I demanded that Tejah be or do things a specific way.

It wasn't that I was wrong about creating a schedule. It wasn't that I was wrong about trying to meet that schedule. Here's what I was wrong about:

Demands create limitations.

The limitation created by my demand — by any demand that any of us have at any time — was to confine my experience to that small slice of reality that said, "This is how things should be."

I limited my experience to the reality of what I wanted. I could not embrace the unfolding reality of what was. I grew frustrated and angry. I blamed others — in this example, my granddaughter.

Opportunities for transformation occur in the most mundane aspects of our life. You can't get more mundane than trying to shuttle kids and dogs out of the door and into the car on time.

Why we have demands

Remember there are two critical differences between a true need and a demand.

1. A true need arises from a place of integrated awareness. It arises with an understanding of what is essential to make us materially and spiritually happy, holy, healthy, and wealthy.

2. A true need can be met but a demand can never be met. Ever.

There are 3 reasons a *true need* converts into a demand.

1. We are unsure what are our needs are.

2. We are dedicated to blaming others for our life experiences.

3. We are unable to believe that we deserve what we long for.

"Will" versus "Can" Helps Us Distinguish between a True Need and a Demand

Here is the question that helps clarify what is a *true need* and what is a *demand*:

Can my expectation or my desire be met?

Versus

Will my expectation or my desire be met?

Consider:

If a desire <u>*can* be met</u> — even if the circumstances in that moment don't support that happening — it is indeed a *true need*.

Because the desire, the longing, or the expectation can be met in some moment — even if it's not this precise moment — that moment can come.

If, on the other hand, for some reason our desire <u>will not be met</u>, that desire or expectation becomes a demand.

The reasons our desires are not met.

Perhaps we have an unevolved child consciousness that is unable to even know what our needs are. Perhaps we're attached to blame and no matter what we would rather blame than heal. Or we just can't see or believe that our desire could be met. We believe we don't deserve it.

This entire dynamic of needs vs demands is not about someone else's ability to respond (though that is certainly a gracious benefit for our life). It's more about our ability to believe, to know, to trust that we have the capacity to receive.

We spend most of the time unaware of our true needs. Instead, our lives are driven by demands on ourselves and others.

Understanding a True Need as a Healing Response to Our Demands - part 1

There are three criteria to have a true need met:

1. An identification of the need.
2. The opportunity to receive. Letting go of blame.
3. The ability to receive. We are worthy of it.

Our desires and expectations can arise from any aspect of our life: love, listening, safety, support — anything. It could be an existential, human, or material need. It could be a spoken or unspoken desire.

A Demand

Here are a few mundane examples of demands that can occur in our day to day life.

In these examples, the need is identified. There is the opportunity to receive, but there is an inability to receive.

Asker: I need to be loved.
Giver: I love you.
Asker: No, you don't, because if you did then you would _____.

This becomes a demand, since the need to be loved <u>will</u> not be met.

Asker: I need a foot rub.
Giver: I always give you foot rubs.
Asker: No, you don't.

Asker: I need you to be in the car at 9 A.M.
Giver: [reality takes over]
Asker: [mad, frustrated, etc.] Get in the car!

Of course, Givers can participate equally in the dynamics of sabotaging a *true need* and converting it into a demand.

Asker: I need you to listen to me.
Giver: You never listen to me.

Pick one example of this dynamic in your life. Write it in your journal.

In a demand, we become fixated on what we are *not* getting — on what the other is *not* giving. We focus on how distraught we are or how much pain we are in. We can't put aside the story of why we are not getting what we desire.

Time snapped back to its normal pace. No more than a couple seconds had passed. I heard the birds chirp, twitter, and thrill their morning symphony. The dog ran past. My daughter was getting into the minivan. Tejah popped out of her disappointment and bustled off, seemingly unphased.

Yet I felt pain. The belief that a demand could make my life easier and better was no longer valid. Demands create tension in my body. Demands create push in my actions. Demands plant controlling thoughts in my mind. They create pain in my relationships.

This became a moment of awareness. Awareness is the first step on the path towards enlightenment. The ability to respond is the second step.

Understanding a True Need as a Healing Response to Our Demands - part 2

There are three criteria to have a true need met:

1. An identification of the need.
2. The opportunity to receive. Letting go of blame.
3. The ability to receive. We are worthy of it.

Here are a few examples of a true need.

Asker: I need to be loved.
Giver: I love you.
Asker: Thank you.

The need is clear. There is an opportunity to receive (the Giver is responsive). The Asker can receive.

Asker: I need to be heard.

Giver: I hear you.
Asker: Thank you.

Asker: I need support.
Giver: I am here for you.
Asker: Thank you.

Asker: I need a beer.
Giver: Here you go.
Asker: Thanks.

In the example with Tejah, my true need was *not* that we leave by 9 AM.

My true need was to feel at ease in moments when life is not what I expected.

That's the Great Quest. That's the evolutionary journey my soul longs for. That's what I don't know how to do. That was the true need usurped by the demand that "only if" someone or some facet of life — or even some aspect of myself — were different, things would be easier or better.

Because I was unable to feel at ease when my demands weren't met by others, I blamed my granddaughter. On the surface, I blamed her for being late. Below the surface, I blamed her for how I felt: frustrated and tense.

Expressing frustration with my granddaughter was just a minor event. It was a small breadcrumb of all the life experiences I have had. It barely rises to the level of profound. It was a moment I could have been passed over as easily as I pass over all the other moments in my day.

But the universe is patient. It offers breadcrumbs that lead us on our path.

It offers such opportunities to reflect far more often than we know. Had I not witnessed the impact of my demand; the universe would have offered me another opportunity to witness it. Had I not witnessed the pain my demand caused on that soft, warm summer morning, the universe would have offered me another opportunity, and then another, and then another to sharpen my awareness.

The universe patiently invites all of us to take our first step on the path towards enlightenment until we do.

Practice:

The concepts in this chapter are challenging. Dedicate some time to determining whether your longing is a true need which can be met, or a demand that cannot be met.

In your journal, replicate the demand cycle and fill in the blanks for yourself.

Here is a diagram of the demand cycle. Start with "My demand is."

This is how the demand cycle plays out in relationships:

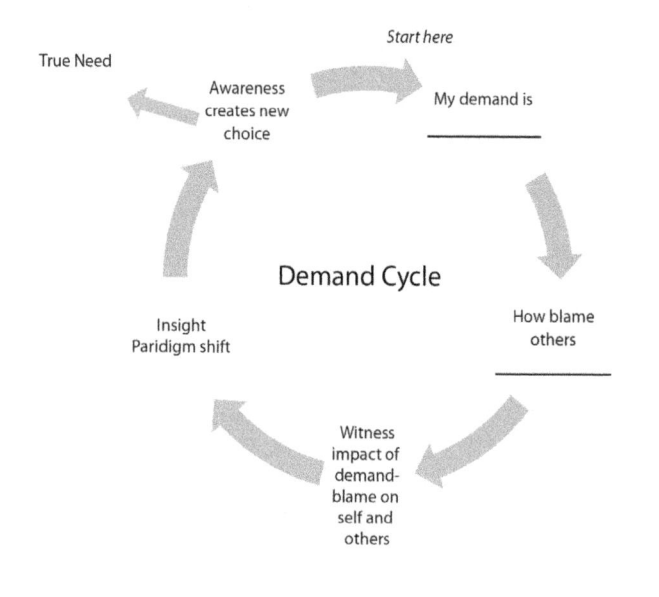

We project our demand onto another person. We insist, directly or subtly, that they do it for us or give it to us. When they don't — and, just in case you haven't already learned this lesson, they never do — we get to blame them for how we feel or how our life plays out.

The Takeaway

The essence of this paradigm is that a true need <u>can</u> be met, a demand <u>will never</u> be met.

Demands create tension in our body, push in actions and controlling thoughts in our minds. They create pain in our relationships.

14

Going Beyond Getting Over It

I'm so hard pressed, my mind tied up in knots,
I keep recycling the same old thoughts.

—Bob Dylan

I WALKED TO my car through the ever-present mist of the Seattle night. The November chill seeped into my bones. It compounded my irritation. Ending a relationship was one thing; I could get over that. In fact, I kept telling myself, I was already over it.

I was tired and hungry. It was late. I just wanted to go home.

But I couldn't.

I paused. I stomped my foot in frustration. I shook my fist towards the heavens. "This is not right. This is not what I want!"

The home I knew wasn't there anymore. Finding myself without a home to go home to was altogether a different matter than finding myself out of a relationship.

I felt conflicted. I was depressed and in angst. I kept telling myself, "You've got to get over this."

At some point in our lives, every one of us has uttered these words:

- I'm over that.

- I've moved on.

- I've dealt with that.

- I don't think about it.

- It doesn't bother me.

- I let it go.

As familiar as these sentiments are, have you ever wondered where it goes when we let go of it? Perhaps it evaporates into the cosmos. Perhaps we store it in the basement of our subconscious.

Maybe it just runs endless loops through our mind.

Consider the likelihood that it ends up somewhere in our physical body or a dusty recess of our psyche. Consider the likelihood that whatever it is that we claim no longer bothers us finds its way into our heart, gallbladder, belly, or neck. Consider the possibility that whatever we have told ourselves we have moved on from manifests as an ache, tension, tic, or anxiety that has an irksome familiarity.

Why We Want to "Get Over" Something

It's fair to say that we put little effort into moving on from something that is pleasurable.

But when we are in pain, our efforts to get over or let go of something are well-intended attempts to stop the angst we are in. When we are in pain, we are driven to alleviate it. This is a natural physiological reaction. Our bodies react to pain. When we stub a toe, we pull back. If we touch something sharp, we recoil. If someone yells at us, we pull away. With pain that is chronic, we withdraw our energy and consciousness — whether from a painful part of our body or from a painful part of our life.

In the realm of relationships, common symptoms that motivate our desire to move on include pain that tightens our gut, repetitive thoughts that distracts our mind, and emotions that create sadness, anger, or frustration. This angst is directly correlated with the person, thing, or event we are trying to let go of.

Interestingly, this pain we experience is not external. Instead, it is embedded in the most intimate recesses of our own psyche.

No wonder we want to get over it.

We hope that if we move on, if we separate from the person or event, we will be in less pain. But our efforts are incomplete. Letting go of something alleviates — but does not resolve — the root of our pain.

Our goal in transformational work is to heal the pain we are experiencing. The goal of a mindful life is to *integrate* our experiences — not *separate from* them.

Separating is, at times, an essential tool. After all, we don't want to rent too much space in our brains and body for things, people, and events that no longer serve us. And, as we just reminded ourselves, it's normal to withdraw from a painful stimulus.

In acute pain, our consciousness initially moves towards the pain. This allows us to assess and respond — usually by withdrawing.

In chronic pain, our consciousness withdraws. This is one of the reasons it is difficult to heal chronic physical or emotional pain.

Because we have done our best to separate from it, it's harder for us to assess and respond. We know that energy follows consciousness. We know that energy is essential for healing. So, if we withdraw our consciousness and energy away from an area — be that in our body or in our lives — our ability to heal is all that more difficult.

Letting go of it, getting over it, and separating from it all have places in our dualistic world. But what if we could go a step further? What if we could go beyond getting over it?

Beyond Getting Over It

In this paradigm, let's consider that we never really get over anything. We never really let something go. We might store it, contain it, or forget it. We could convince ourselves it doesn't bother us. We may leave it behind or manage it.

At least for a while

All of us, at some point have — with the best of intentions — said, "I'm over it" only to have "it" resurface as a sensation, a feeling, or a memory.

What we resist persists.

When you want to let go of something — a past relationship, negative habits or self-talk, physical or emotional pain — you risk creating a dualistic situation in which two things exist:

1. The person, pain, or experience we want to get over.

2. You.

The trauma becomes something we try to separate from. It is painful. We believe that if we separate from it or let it go, we will suffer less pain. Yet in doing so, we reinforce the very nature of duality. Dualism is a doctrine that states the universe is under the dominion of two opposing principles. Classically, we define the principles as good and evil.

When we try to let something go, we create an "us" and we create an "it".

Through dualism, we conclude that we are good. The obvious corollary is that what we want to let go of must be evil. We define it as evil because it isn't us, and we are the good side of duality.

Of course, sometimes we invert these roles. When we blame ourselves, we are the evil side of the duality and thus what we want to let go of must be good.

A foundational truth of duality is that as long as one aspect of the duality exists, the other aspect of the duality exists.

In fact, each opposing aspect exists solely because the other exists. Therefore, as long as there is something we want to let go of, it will exist as long as we exist. The reverse also is true: as long as we exist, what we want to let go of will exist.

We are quite familiar with the concept of duality in our daily life. Visually, it's often illustrated with the classic yin and yang symbol. We all understand the concept of good because we have its opposite to compare. We understand camaraderie and bright, warm sunlight because we know what it is to be cold and alone in the dark. Our physical world continuously reflects duality — we call it day and night. We call it light and dark. Random acts of kindness and genocide.

The evolutionary gift of incarnating into a world of duality is that we get to learn, grow, and evolve. "So what?" you may react. Evolving as an individual in this incarnation is not a requirement. It's an opportunity. It's an opportunity to transform and deepen mindfulness.

Our external physical world reflects that which exists in the depth and breadth of our own psyche as well as in the collective consciousness of all humanity. Without this reflection from the external world, how would we see the effects of our thoughts and actions?

We project the duality that resides within us out onto the world. Each of us is good and creates light that shines on our fellow humans. Each of us is evil and creates darkness on the face of the earth. Perhaps evil is a strong image here. Yet if we define evil as causing harm, then surely, we must admit that somewhere along this incarnational journey we have — knowingly or not — caused harm.

On this planet, in this incarnation, duality is a tool created by the greater powers of the universe to allow us a life in which we are able to experience an exceptionally rapid learning curve.

Consider that there are worlds of incarnation that have no duality. In these worlds, there may be just light or just darkness. Just love or just pain. There are worlds made of thick rock where consciousness incarnates with the sole purpose to experience density. The evolutionary learning curve on these worlds, though profound unto themselves, is not as rapid as on the blue planet Earth.

Here, in a single lifetime, we experience both the absolute bliss of love, pleasure, and beauty, and the absolute devastation of loss, pain, and ugliness. This external reflection of our dualistic life allows us to see and experience our internal duality. This reflection offers us a way to heal and integrate the duality within us.

With the reflection of the physical world and the crucible of relationships, we can begin the healing process, transform our lives, and live mindfully.

Integration

Instead of letting go and separating, the goal in transformational work and mindful living is integration. In integration, the duality of opposites ceases to exist.

Integration is the ability to combine and coordinate separate parts or elements into a unified whole.

In integration there is no longer an us and a them. There is no longer a good and an evil. There is great healing potential in the act of integration. In integration, the emotional pain and the negative charge of separation dissolves.

What would it be like to integrate whatever it is we are trying to get over?

I got into my old Subaru, cranked it over, and let it run until the defroster cleared the foggy windows. I drove through the night, through rain-blurred streets, to my brother's house and my bedroom in the basement. Sleep was my favorite respite. It allowed me to escape the battering I gave myself: "If only I had…." It allowed me to escape the endless recycling of negative thoughts that filled my waking hours: "If only they hadn't…."

Each morning, I would startle awake to a freight train of angst and anxiety. My body would tense, my stomach would tighten, and my energy would drain even before I put my feet on the floor. I did get up. I was cold and weary. Always. I couldn't wait to get back into the car and blast the heat. Would I ever feel warm in Seattle?

I grabbed some granola and off I drove. The world of rain distorted traffic with streaks of red in a sea of grey seemed like a telling reflection of my internal experience.

It was on one of those morning commutes that I began to realize the obvious. I'd spent so much effort trying to get over her and so much effort trying to separate from my pain that I had made her and it all-consuming. I had made it that much more powerful.

My most obvious realization was simple. It was void of earth-shaking insights or lightning bolts of wisdom. My realization was actually a choice.

A choice that — like all transformational moments — was not of habit.

A choice that was not particularly easy, but certainly not complicated. I realized the obvious:

I could tell myself kind things just as readily as I had been hammering myself with criticism.

As I did this, over days and weeks, slowly and with practice, I noticed that my body was less tense. My stomach began working again — or, at least, it stopped tugging at my attention with pain. I began to let words like *forgive* and *breathe* float through my consciousness. "I forgive you" became my mantra.

Forgiveness

Initially, I focused my forgiveness outward on those who had done me wrong.

"Forgive them, for they know not what they do" was my starting point. I wish, as modeled by Jesus on the cross, I could say that I came from a place of mercy and love. But, with honest reflection, I came from a place of pity and scorn. Instead of putting my focus on "forgive them," I put my focus on "they know not what they do" because they were stupid jerks.

I knew this to be true because my initial effort to forgive arose from my mind, not my heart. And it didn't really change my angst. A tincture of time was a critical factor. "I forgive you" rang hollow at first. It was only once I engaged my heart that my mantras of forgiveness became a salve that anointed my wounds.

Soon, what I call Realization of the Obvious, Round Two arose within me. "I forgive you." I realized that my mantra was not directed outward. Instead, I was talking directly to myself. I began to understand the true practice of forgiveness.

The foundation of forgiveness was not for me to forgive another, but for me to forgive myself.

"I forgive you" was my soul speaking to my ego and offering vespers to soothe my angst.

Practice:

The mantra "I forgive you" is powerful. The following practice helps make it an even more heartfelt experience.

The great thing about mantras is that they can be done in any setting at any time. Standing in line at the grocery store. Stuck in traffic. Sitting in contemplation. Every moment is a ripe experience for your mantra. The key to making the "I forgive you" mantra a heartfelt experience is a two-fold process.

First, breathe gently and deeply. Allow your belly and chest to expand. Imagine the air filling your chest and heart space. This creates a bit of room in a heart that may be cramped or tight.

Second, the mantra "I forgive you" is not directional. You do not send or direct it at a person. It is not "for" anyone. It wells up from deep within our innermost being and radiates out, like heat from an old steam radiator.

Forgiveness is a state of being that has no attachment to a result.

The medicinal benefit of forgiveness occurs as it permeates, penetrates, infuses, and informs our body-mind and our spirit.

Over time and with heartfelt practice, I began to feel less torn apart and more whole. It was as though I took a step inward and found myself again. As though I took a step back and could see the big picture.

This was the beginning of my healing process. This was the beginning of integrating my painful experience.

The Healing Approach

Integration means that there is no it, him, or her to get over because the pain we desire to let go of is in us.

Habitually, we carry the false belief that if we separate discordant experiences and parts of ourselves, we will stop our pain. As we do so, we discover that pretty soon we have tucked away or split off so many pieces it becomes exceedingly difficult to feel whole.

In integration there is no separation. There is no hiding of unpleasant or painful experiences in our subconsciousness or our physical body or heart or belly or gallbladder.

Integration is the opposite of dualism. Integration is to claim — in fact, to *embrace* — those parts of ourselves that we have dissociated with.

What we desire to get over is not the person or experience. It is the painful feeling in our own physical and emotional body. We correlate that pain with a person or experience. We believe that if we are able to let the person go or get over the experience, we will escape that pain.

Integration is challenging, but not complicated.

Here is a two-step framework to go from separation to integration:

First, witness the thought or the feeling that evokes pain.

Second, make a choice that — like all transformational moments — is not of habit.

Practice:

Let's say you want to get over a pattern of negative self-talk.

Perhaps in your daily routine you tell yourself how you are no good, or a failure, or how you are fat or ugly. We degrade ourselves in any number of a thousand different ways.

And, as if this weren't unhealthy enough, we then add to the pain by judging ourselves for how we degrade ourselves. We feel bad about our negative self-talk. In essence, we tell ourselves we're a loser for feeling like a loser.

This becomes a downward spiral. It creates more pain that we then try to get over. Our best efforts might include counseling, classes, workshops, retreats, reading self-help books, and spiritual instruction. We go on diets and treat ourselves to sweets. We do therapy or buy new clothes.

There's nothing wrong with any of these approaches. In our quest for a mindful life, it is vital to be aware of our actions. The essential question is, "Does this action separate or integrate?"

In your journal, complete this sentence with as many practices as you can think of:

When I am in pain or angst, I tend to _____, _____, and _____.

Now, circle the practices that integrate.

And draw a line through the practices that separate.

Integrating Painful Experiences

A child falls and skins her knees. She is in pain on two levels: physical and emotional.

My guess is that the last time you fell and had a road rash, it hurt. In addition to the physical pain, the fall can cause mental pain, as would any sudden, out-of-control moment.

This child comes to you in tears. She's catching her breath and obviously in distress.

What is your response?

One response may be to say, "Oh, it's all right. It's just a little scrape. Don't cry. Everything is going to be all right. Let's get some ice cream and make it all right."

This approach, though well-intended, has the effect of separating the child from the experience. Pain bad, child good.

It also has the unintended outcome of denying the child's experience of reality. She is in pain. You are telling her that she is not.

It also models a reaction to pain that emphasizes distraction or treating ourselves to a reward. Could there be a correlation between this modeling for children and, as adults, seeking medication, drugs, or alcohol to distract or deny our experiences?

An integrative response looks different.

This child comes to you in tears, catching her breath, obviously in distress. You hold the child with a heart connection and affirm her experience: "Wow, I see that you are in pain. I bet that hurt. If I fell like that, I would hurt also. I love you. I love your knees."

Integrating painful experiences follows a two-step process.

First, become the unbiased witness:

- I see you are hurt.

- Here is that negative self-talk.

- My belly tightens whenever I think of what happened.

This takes practice. Becoming the witness is essential to transformational work and a mindful life. As an unbiased witness, we observe but do not judge. An unbiased witness experiences the experience while observing the experience. It is not a place of detachment but a state of expanded awareness.

Witnessing anger allows me to be angry while I observe the anger and the impact it has on me and my surroundings. "I feel pressure in my chest, my heart is pounding, and I want to blame everybody for everything... hmmm... I am in the witness role."

I am still angry, but I am also in the witness role.

Commit to spend some time in the witness role. You do it all the time anyway. Just notice when you are hungry, tired, cranky, happy, or anxious. These are simple ways we witness our state of being.

Second, make a conscious choice:

The second step of integrating painful experiences is when choice comes in. Choice is the hallmark of enlightenment, transformation, and creating a mindful life. When integrating a painful experience, we choose to observe and learn from the experience so we can make it part of us, instead of choosing to isolate and segregate it.

Within the witness role is the ability to observe in our physical body how it feels to participate in separation and trying to get over, for example, pain from a fall, a downward spiral of negative self-talk, or "that" relationship. Choice places us on the threshold of transformation.

Negative self-talk, skinning our knee, or a traumatic break-up is painful. Instead of pushing away that pain, our conscious choice is to:

- Witness it.
- Embrace it.
- Integrate it.

As we practice witnessing, embracing, and integrating painful experiences, we stop dissociating and separating off parts of our self. We begin to heal. We begin to become whole.

We can choose to begin to integrate this often-intolerable pain, as a kind and patient parent would hold a hurt child, enfolding them into loving and accepting arms. As we do this, we begin to dissolve the duality that has been holding this painful pattern in place.

This practice of witnessing, embracing, and integrating takes positive intention and practice. It takes mindfulness and heart.

Another example is one I see in my medical practice as an acupuncturist:

- It's just my dumb knee acting up again.
- My neck is really bad.
- It's this stupid back pain — it never goes away.

You want to get over your dumb knee or your stupid back pain. Acupuncture is a highly effective modality. In most cases, it will remedy the pain. However, it cannot remedy the dualism created when you try to separate and get over the pain.

The two steps of a mindful approach are witnessing it and choosing to integrate it instead of separating it from the rest of your experience.

In the first step, you witness the relationship between you and your pain. What are your thoughts and feelings about it? Hate, anger, or frustration? Understandably so — there is no judgment here. Just become the witness of that dynamic with your pain.

In the second step, make a choice. Does that relationship of hate, anger, or frustration create a unified field of healing? Hate, anger, and frustration are emotions of separation. Integration, on the other hand, enfolds. It applies love, acceptance, and forgiveness to the experience.

What if you placed your hand on your painful body part and said:

- I love you.
- I forgive you.
- I hold you as I would hold a hurt child — with patience and compassion.

After you do this, pick up the phone and make an appointment for some acupuncture treatments.

The Takeaway

This is a healing approach. The experience becomes less about who or what we want to get over. It becomes more about healing and transforming the pain we feel. We heal the pain not by separating from it and creating a duality, but by integrating it, embracing it, forgiving it, and compassionately holding it. As we do this, we begin to create a sense of wholeness in ourselves.

PART FIVE

Mundane Life as An
Enlightened Adventure

15

Thinkers, Feelers, and Doers

Experience is not what happens to a man;
it is what a man does with what happens to him.

—Aldous Huxley

I WAS RUDDERLESS in a swirling sea of change when I landed at the door of the local psychiatrist. The office was comfortable enough. It had the requisite leather couch, wing-backed chair, and glass-top table with a few *Woman's Day* magazines neatly stacked next to a potted prayer plant. The plant drooped. It needed water.

"How appropriate," I thought to myself. "How analogous to my situation."

The irony was not lost on me. I had come to the end of my coping capabilities. I'd made the appointment with hope this psychiatrist would be the person who would erase my pain. A sudden and traumatic relationship break-up came in the middle of my master's program. I found myself in search of a place to live while traveling 100 miles to school and back on a weekly basis.

I only saw the therapist once. I have no recollection of his name. But to this day, I remember one very important thing he said. I was sharing the depth of my situation and my befuddlement about how someone could make choices that were foreign to my nature.

He said, "She doesn't think like you do."

This was a light bulb moment in an otherwise dark day of my life. It had never crossed my mind that others did not think the way I did. I am a reason-oriented person. I hold good, logical streams of thought with which I am able to make sense of my world.

I assumed everyone saw and navigated the world that way. I mean, how could they not? What other way could they do it?

Because my belief system held firm to this precept, I was unable to imagine a reality in which this paradigm doesn't exist.

The more strongly we hold a belief system, the more force must be applied to break us free from, or wake us to, the limitations of that belief.

I believed that everyone thinks and processes reality as I do. If they reached conclusions different than I did, it was simply because they did not fully understand. With a bit of logical conversation, they would understand and come to the same conclusions as I did.

This sounds childlike and immature, doesn't it? But, then, that is the nature of our belief systems. They arise from our child consciousness. They develop and are set into place from our childhood experiences. They harden into the matrix of our cellular structure. Our behaviors, driven by our belief systems, are played and replayed through our lives until a course correction breaks the spell.

Life is full of course corrections. A mindful life has no fewer and no more course corrections then an unmindful life.

There is a gift in the pain that a course correction inflicts. That gift is the shattering of our limiting beliefs. This shattering becomes an evolutionary opportunity. It allows us to broaden how we define ourselves and view our world. This broadens how we interact with our world.

Though I was not feeling grateful during that shattered phase of my life, I am certainly grateful now. I swept up the pieces of that shattered belief system, planted them in the soil of my psyche, and let them germinate for about ten years.

I was in my mid-30's when this course correction challenged my belief that everyone in the world thinks as I think. And if that belief was no longer valid, then it would also make sense that not everyone feels the way I feel or acts the way I act. In fact, it became clear to me that some of us predominantly *think* our way through life, some of us *feel* our way through life, and others of us *do*, or act, as our primary method of navigating the challenges and opportunities placed before us.

Thinkers, Feelers, and Doers.

These designations reflect the most comfortable mode in which we interface with the world.

These modes, as with all our behavioral habits, are developed in the first few years of life. As children, in response to events in our environment, we begin to moderate behavior with the hope that doing so will keep us safe.

Initially, it is trial and error. How many times do we touch a hot stove before we create a behavior that not only avoids hot stoves but gives us the impulse to cautiously approach any stove for the rest of our lives, feeling with our hand to see if it is hot?

How many times do my feelings get discounted and belittled before I realize that thinking is a safer mode of behavior than feeling?

I grew up in an environment in which expressing emotions was seen as weak. Emotions had little value. I quickly learned (subconsciously) that to survive in my family dynamics, I needed to develop a rational, logical, mental approach. Figuring out what I needed to do to avoid my father's discipline became paramount. Figuring out what I needed to do to take care of my mother became a theme. Thinking became my modus operandi.

Another child in the same environment, governed by the laws of karma and free will, might have come to a different conclusion. Another child might forego the thinking mode to navigate their experience with feeling or by doing.

From these childhood patterns, we develop behavior that becomes our *modus operandi*, or MO, through our lives. Habitually, we will each favor one of these modes — Thinker, Feeler, Doer — though all modes can be available at a moment's notice, should we desire (with mindfulness or not) to use them.

There is nothing inherently wrong or bad with any of these modes. In fact, they helped us navigate and survive childhood. But in the artful journey of personal transformation, it is wholeness that we seek. In the paradigm of Thinkers, Feelers, and Doers, wholeness would necessitate not only the ability to access all three modes with choice and consciousness, but to move through life and engage relationships with all three modes in balance more and more of the time.

Identifying our mode and someone else's mode is exceptionally empowering.

I am a Thinker. I synchronize easily and well with other Thinkers because our relational MO is harmonically similar. As for Doers, I am able to engage with others who operate in that mode because I can — in addition to thinking my way through life — create action that enables me to manifest my goals. I sync less well with Feelers.

With this understanding and a bit of mindfulness, I am able to do two empowering things:

1. Release the demand that the person I am in relationship with will be different (they won't) and release the expectation that they be like me (remember my shattered belief that others think as I think).

2. With a little practice, I can modulate my energy and consciousness to open my heart and emotional centers to make myself harmonically compatible with the Feeler archetype.

As I do this, with awareness, I create synchronization between me and those of the Feeler mode. I intentionally move out of my habitual Thinker pattern and expanded my repertoire to include the emotional realm of Feelers. As I do so, I feel connected and present. I feel more in balance. Feelers, sensing some compassionate harmonic induction in me, begin to feel safe. By doing so, I have successfully deepened my relationship.

If I were to talk strictly logic to a Feeler, we would be on two different planes. Our communication would not — in fact, could not — synchronize. Studies by Dr. Albert Mehrabian, author of *Silent Messages*, concluded that 7% of any message is conveyed through words, 38% through certain vocal elements, and 55% through nonverbal elements (facial expressions, gestures, posture, etc.).

It is not what I say that allows me to communicate with others. It is the energy behind what I say. I need to approach from a feeling mode before the Feeler archetype can fully comprehend what I am communicating.

Of course, the reverse is true. When someone communicates exclusively about feelings, it will not connect well with the logical person that I am. When someone says, "It just feels right," I respond, "Well, does it make sense?"

Observing the Different Modes

Thinkers

If you were to observe a group of Thinkers, you would notice that they are very mental. The upper parts of their bodies, especially their heads and hands, would be very active. The realm of the Thinker is structured, clear, rigid, and linear. Thinkers process their world quickly and sharply, like the ring of church bells on a clear crisp autumn night.

Feelers

In observing Feelers, you would notice that their energy is softer. It is more active in the front of their bodies, mostly centered around the heart. Feelers present their energy and MO of interfacing with the world based on the soft, amorphous, ever-changing emotional realm. Feelers process their world more slowly than Thinkers and Doers, as though things are moving through fluid. Feelers notice what is happening on the unspoken level. They are keyed into the emotional energy that is present behind the words being spoken. Feelers take their time in processing their world, but in slowing things, what they bring forward is deep, rich, and insightful.

Doers

The best example of Doers is a work or construction crew. They lean forward, shovels in hand, ready to start with strong backs and shoulders. Anyone with this physical and energy dynamic is a Doer. Doers are ready to lead or to follow as long as action is occurring.

Their energy and MO tend to be dense in the upper part of their torso. They are physically solid, like the trunk of a towering evergreen tree. When communicating, they will often lean towards you to ensure that you are getting the full forward movement of what they are saying.

Here are some further ways to uncover your relational mode:

Observe how decisions are made. Do you, or does the other:

- Consider all the pros and cons, research the options, and talk to people or search the internet for information?

- Talk about what feels right, even if it doesn't appear logical?

- Chomp at the bit to get something done even before contemplating all the variables?

When speaking, what language do you or the other use?

- "I think I'll have ice cream."

- "I feel like some ice cream."

- "I'm going to drive to the store and buy enough ice cream for the next two weeks."

I have a friend who is a Feeler. She was married to a Doer. He was always off on some work project or bike race or hunting trip. She desired a heartfelt emotional connection.

Though he was aware of her need, he was unaware of how to meet it. Had he had the tools and the willingness to apply them, he would have been able to hold his wife (physically and energetically) on an emotional/feeling level. Without stopping or repressing his Doer MO, he could have expanded his repertoire to include the emotional realm. This would have deepened their ability to meet each other even though their modes are different.

Of course, the Feeler could also expand her repertoire to hold the Doer archetype. The Doer language is one of action. By reflecting the value of their actions, and by acting, the Feeler begins to meet the Doer in his world. It could be as simple as, "I see that you cut the grass and raked the leaves. It looks great. Thanks for how much you do for us."

The goal in mindfulness is balance. There is nothing inherently wrong with any of the modes. With consciousness, we can modulate our relational mode. Modulation brings balance and the ability to deepen relationships with people who are living from their own favorite relational mode.

Expanding our Repertoire

Feelers

To move into the Feeler realm, we need to move our consciousness into the soft, vulnerable aspects of our physical and emotional body centered at our heart. Energy follows consciousness. As we open our heart, we automatically move into the Feeler realm.

One way to open your heart is to hold in your consciousness someone or something you love. Take your time. Perhaps a grandchild, your daughter, or your dog. When you feel a softening or even a pressure in your chest, you know you are on track.

As you do this, things actually feel as though they have slowed. You will notice the profound effect it has on the person you are relating to. They will soften, and the room you are in will soften as well.

Doers

To move into the Doer realm, create action. To create action, lift your shoulders, open your stance, and place your hands on your hips. Stand like Superman or Wonder Woman. Or raise your hands over your head as though you just scored the winning goal in the World Cup. This will activate your Doer energies.

Hold in your consciousness strength and stamina to achieve your goals. "I can" is a useful mantra. You will feel a thickening or expansiveness through your upper back and shoulders. From this place, you become a leader or a willing follower. People will notice you.

Held in balance, this Doer mode brings a high degree of respect from others.

Thinkers

To move into the Thinker realm, open and relax your throat. Visualize clarity and the unfolding of events in a linear fashion: First A, then B, then C. 1 + 1 = 2. 2 + 2 = 4.

Thinkers are "bright" because the spark and activity in their mental body generates a lot of energy. Hold in your consciousness brightness, clarity, order, and a stepwise progression. "I can figure it out," is a useful mantra. As you do this, your mind becomes clear. Your consciousness becomes contemplative. Answers appear not because Thinkers go after answers, but because the infinite possibilities that abound in the universe come to them.

People look to Thinkers to deepen their understanding of, well, just about anything. Thinkers create a framework for concepts and can bring clarity to a partnership or group.

The Takeaway

A mindful life encompasses a growing awareness of who we are and how we interface with others. Being aware of our relational mode is an exceptionally powerful tool in helping us deepen our relationships.

Our first step is to discover our own mode. The next step is to practice bringing balance to our modes so we can harmonize with someone in any of the other modes. This is fun to practice, has no downside, and can be exceptionally useful in enhancing both personal and professional relationships.

16

Elevator

Too often we underestimate the power of a touch,
a smile, a kind word, a listening ear, an honest
compliment, or the smallest act of caring, all of
which have the potential to turn a life around.

—Leo Buscaglia

AFTER A FULL day teaching, I found the hum and upward movement of the elevator relaxing to my body and mind. The elevator came to a stop on the top floor. The doors opened. I was just about to step off when I noticed a young boy and his father waiting to get on. With bright excitement in his voice, the boy respectfully asked, "Hey mister, is this elevator going down?"

The enthusiasm in this young boy's voice stirred me from my end of the workday daze. As I stepped into the hallway, I realized how profoundly I was affected by his simple question.

I had to smile. We were on the top floor. Where else could that elevator go but down? And then I realized why I was so deeply affected:

Just because I know something and it is obvious to me, doesn't mean it is so obvious to someone else.

I thought of how much of the time I spend assuming others see, believe, and experience the world as I do. How limiting that is for me. I miss out on the variety and multitude of ways this ever-evolving experiment of life can be lived.

When I expand beyond my own view of how the world is and consciously experience another's point of view, I find myself in much deeper contact. I find myself feeling much more compassionate. If the goal of a mindful life is to become more aware of ourselves and our relationships, this young boy's innocent question presented me with a profound gift. He evoked in me a cascade of feelings, the most predominant one being compassion. He allowed me to remind myself to feel the freedom of not having to know the answer, even if that answer is obvious to everyone else. And he beautifully modeled with pure joy what it is to be curious in the present moment.

The Takeaway

One of the things we come to understand from deep transformational work is that the external environment will present to us, on a surprisingly regular basis, those things which we need to learn in our life's evolutionary journey. Carl Jung called it synchronicity.

The great photographer Ansel Adams was fond of saying, "The world presents to a prepared mind."

I simply refer to it as paying attention. I allow the experiences of my day to mean something even if, on the surface, the events seem small and unimportant.

17

A Premonition

*The fog comes on little cat feet. It sits looking over harbor
and city on silent haunches and then moves on.*

—Carl Sandburg

THIS PREMONITION, LIKE most premonitions, settled on me like the
evening fog. It advanced quietly and softly, chillingly undeterred.

Like fog, premonitions seem to behave independently of the
laws of nature. They seep, roll, penetrate, lift, hang, and loom. They
bear down with omnipresence. They appear from nowhere, infiltrate
us, and then move on. They can't be touched, but they can be felt. If
fog had a sound and a feel, this oncoming premonition was a freight
train barreling down the tracks.

This premonition carried the foreboding sense of doom. It was
a foreboding feeling of death, of a life taken by the hand of fate in
some traumatic way. My diligent attempts to push this feeling away

were futile. I was no more successful than had I tried to hold the fog in my hands.

Not all premonitions are foreboding. The phone rings and you know immediately who it is. An old friend you haven't seen in months pops into your head and you run into that friend later that day. Driving home at night, with no one around, you follow an irrational impulse and move from the right lane to the left as you round a bend. There, on the right side of the road, is a four-point buck. You certainly would have hit it, had you not changed lanes.

Premonitions come to us in a variety of ways. A voice or vision. A gut feeling. A knowing that bypasses the thought process. Premonitions are not that unusual; they happen all the time.

Premonitions are just one way that the universe communicates with us.

These visions, insights, voices, or gut feelings beckon us to live more mindfully. They offer us an opportunity to synchronize with the pulse of the universe. They offer us a focal point to expand our consciousness. Premonitions may offer deep, life-altering insight. They might be just an interesting form of guidance.

Regardless, premonitions are a powerful way of connecting, confirming and communicating with the universe and the mysteries therein.

I was on a road trip with a friend. It was a simple trip to the coast on a busy holiday weekend. We arrived at our lodge early. After settling in, we decided to head back out to catch the sunset from a mountain perch overlooking Puget Sound.

All went smoothly from external appearances. Internally, a fog-like premonition tugged at my psyche. It penetrated deeper into my bones. It created an anxious, bothered, hurried feeling. This freight train of a premonition was approaching fast. It was an overwhelming hum, hiss, and rumble bearing down on my soul.

I thought to myself, "Let's go, do it, and get back. Let the future be now so what I am experiencing in the present can run its course and be done with." What could have been an exceptional experience in a beautiful setting became an anxious, distracted chore.

We got to the trail head, somehow found a parking spot in a jam-packed lot, and headed up the path. Moving away from the hustle-bustle would normally be soothing to my system. But not on this particular evening. Not with this particular premonition.

My companion, sensing something amiss, asked how I was.

"Fine," I said automatically.

Yet inside my chest there was a uniquely new feeling of vacancy, hollow and growing. I was wound up and tense, talking about distracting things like math problems. I was anxious, though not panicky. My breath was short and shallow. I was thoroughly absorbed and interested in this unfolding internal experience.

I had trouble being present with the physical world around me. Energetically, I kept lifting out of my body. I didn't feel as though I was going to drop dead on the trail, but I kept wondering if I was dying.

At that moment, as we hiked the trail, a vortex opened above me. It was grey, swirling, cloudy, and dusty. I felt a strong pulling-up sensation through my physical body. The further I walked, the stronger it got.

My mind tried to rationalize it. It substituted the vision of the dusty vortex with a vision of the great Akashic records, endless tiers of the books of knowledge, spiraling and stretching into infinity. That vision quickly faded, obscured by the swirling maelstrom of the grey dust. The pulling-up sensation continued, stronger through my chest.

We arrived at the lookout. Vistas of the setting sun over waters and islands. The land below with trees and fields. Distant city lights twinkled as the sun's daily performance grew to a close. From our post of rock and trees, the twilight sounds filtered up the hill: chattering birds, squirrels rustling through the dry brush, the hum and swish of the cars below, the gentle breeze. In the distance, a tanker dieseled towards open water.

My partner, sensing my agitation, tried to rub my shoulders, though she soon gave up due to my unresponsive nature. That freight train was still approaching fast.

My action became robotic. I defaulted to either stillness or hyper movement. I walked around, fidgeting, trying to ground but failing. Sitting still, I waited for the universe to shift, waited for something — anything — to relieve this pressure, this pulling sensation, this sense of impending doom.

Any casual observation of our actions would have appeared perfectly normal. A couple watching the sunset, taking pictures, chatting, being silent in the beauty of the setting.

The high wah-wah sound of a siren split the air. Another followed, then another, and another. *Ahooga ahooga ahooga.* Rapid and repetitive, starting at a distance, coming closer and closer. We watched the distant lights flashing from town through field to forest. Police cars and trucks and ambulances raced to a point, then stopped in stillness, congregating out of sight just below our perch.

The sun had set. The sky grew dark. Radiant Venus made her appearance in the western sky. The vacancy in my chest began to fill; the universe had shifted.

We started down the trail. The tail of the dust-devil maelstrom moved away from me into a wider swirling pool. It covered the hill we were on and the road we were heading to.

My demeanor shifted, as though I was relieved of some great unknown burden. The train had passed. It had roared so close I felt the push of air. So close. So fast. But it didn't stop at the platform I was on. It didn't stop for me. Not this time. I realized at that point that I would be an observer, not a passenger.

The twilight sounds once again filled the cool air as we hiked down the hill. I felt the earth beneath my feet. I could take a deep breath.

We neared the trailhead. A symphony of red and blue lights pierced the darkening forest. Around a bend, cresting a few stairs, the scene was one of great action and great stillness. Paramedics and officers dutifully paced the road, marked the site, made decisions. Onlookers froze in shock, unable to move, as if the air around them had become overwhelmingly heavy and thick. The dissipating roar from the train of death had spread through the station. It left only a lingering din in the air.

"She didn't stop in time."

"Got thrown from her bike."

"Hit by another car."

The experience happened before we got there. The scene just confirmed both my experience and the unfolding drama.

I didn't stop. I didn't gawk. I didn't look. I'd already had my experience.

As the ambulance pulled away, a quick glimpse into the bright interior revealed the medics dutifully applying CPR and a line of angels passing the soul to heaven.

The Takeaway

Our sixth sense, second sight, intuition, guidance, or premonitions are a useful aspect of a mindful life and transformational work. It is one of the ways the universe communicates its messages and mysteries.

As we open to these greater mysteries, and give them credence, we create a library of experiences that add to the wisdom we gather on our journey home.

18

Push – Pull – Stop – Neutral

*If you do not change directions, you may
end up where you are heading.*

—Lao Tzu

THE WEATHERED DOCK creaked, splashed, and swayed as I looked
out over the sun-glittered waters of Brigantine Bay. Further across
the mud flats, I saw blue herons strutting and jabbing their beaks
into the brackish lagoon. Seagulls laughed and cried at the passing
Boston whaler, laden heavy with nets and poles and ice chests full
of beer. The tide was in, the wind was smooth, the water was warm.
It was a good day to cast a line or hoist a sail.

Lathered in sunscreen, my hat pulled low, I stepped into the
rocking skiff. I dropped the centerboard, pushed off from the dock,
and pulled the rigging to stiffen the sails. I felt a tug as the main-
mast filled. Nothing could stop me now. My first tack was towards

the tall marsh grass, the boat gliding effortlessly. I used my body as ballast so I could cut closer to the wind. There was only the wind, the water, the boat, and me in the mix. Passionate as to experience, alive in the element of now, I was neutral to any particular outcome.

Life is action, be it in thought or deed. As we navigate life, there are four methods of action that we use to interface with our world:

1. Push
2. Pull
3. Stop
4. Neutral

We are always in one of these modes. They are at play throughout our day. From minor actions:

- I push the skiff away from its moorings.
- I pull the rigging taut.
- I push my way through the crowd.

To habitual patterns we use to navigate our life:

- I pulled and pulled and pleaded until I finally got my way.
- He yelled at me, so I just shut down. Everything just stopped. I couldn't even think.

We all know people that push on us or pull on us. We know those who shut down and stop relating. We know those who can find a place of neutral engagement.

It may be easier to see these actions in others, but they are alive in us as well. Rule one of deepening into a mindful relationship:

Being in relationship is not about the other.

Being in relationship simply gives us the opportunity to practice. Practice love, kindness, forgiveness, patience. Being in relationship offers us the most intimate way we can observe who we are and how our actions impact our material world and the people in it.

If we are observant, we will witness where we hurt, where we heal, where we connect, and where we miss the mark.

In our quest to practice our mindful life, it is essential to become aware of when we are in push, pull, stop, or neutral. There is nothing inherently right or wrong with any of these methods of interaction. Each can be essential at different times. The insight that puts us on the road to enlightenment and mindfulness is to observe the impact of our push, our pull, our stop, and our neutral. Mindfulness lets us discern whether our behavior is useful or counterproductive, and whether it heals or hurts.

Push

Imagine you are late for an appointment. If you hit the lights just right and there is a parking spot out front, you'll arrive on time. Barely.

The car in front of you is slow. Not even the speed limit! "Come on, come on, go faster," you mutter, or yell. You lean forward in the seat, grip the steering wheel, and through will and frustration push and push to get that car to move faster. Your heart races. You're tense.

My guess is that this is not too hard to imagine. The familiarity of this scenario connects us intimately with push.

Pull

Now imagine you are at a restaurant with friends. The waitress delivers the water and rolls. Your ravenous companions devour them in a few minutes. Your day was long, and it didn't include lunch. Your belly rumbles.

You look around for the waitress. You see her a couple tables over. In your mind, you try to get her attention. You raise your hand and cast a metaphorical line to pull her attention towards you. She doesn't notice and heads to the bus tables in the back of the room.

You get up and head to where she is talking with other servers. All the while, you are pulling on her to get her attention. Only when you get within a couple of feet does she look up, smile, and politely ask, "May I help you?"

Stop

I walk into my local bank. They are so darn friendly that it actually irritates me. It's 9:00 AM and they ask how my day is. What do I have planned? Do I like the weather?

All I want to do is to make a deposit.

I feel my body tense. I hold my breath. I just want to make a deposit. I'm not here to chat about my personal life. I'm friendly enough, but I don't want to encourage further dialogue. So, I stop the relational flow. One-word answers, an occasional nod.

When you notice that the person you are talking to has folded their arms across their chest, stiffened a bit, and turned slightly away, you're experiencing an example of stop.

Any time we find ourselves withholding or halting the relational flow, we are in stop.

Neutral

I meet with a friend for a beer. It's easy. We chat. I listen and acknowledge the conversation. He does the same. There is no agenda. There is no time. I'm in the present moment. This is neutral.

I drop the centerboard. The wind tugs the sail. Effortlessly, I cut through the light chop as the spray washes away my identity. I am the boat, I am the water, I am the wind.

I am neutral.

Practice:

This is best practiced with a willing partner.

Stand or sit across from one another at a comfortable distance of about three feet. Designate yourselves as either A or B. Taking turns, one person will be active A, the other will be witness B.

The witness role is neutral, non-reactive, and silently asks the question, "What is here now?" The point of this question is not to get an answer but to deepen curiosity. In the witness or neutral role, you may notice how stimuli in your environment affect you, but you do not react. You only witness it.

Start by taking inventory as we did in Chapter 10 *Taking Inventory*. Notice your breath pattern. Notice any tension and whether you feel grounded. This brings awareness to the baseline of our mind-body connection.

Push: A goes into push mode, mentally and energetically but not physically. Embody the essence of push by recalling the push story in this chapter or imagining another situation in which you push your way towards or past another person.

Do this for 15 seconds or so.

Did you notice the impact that push had on you? Did it have an impact on your partner that you noticed or that your partner can share with you? Perhaps more importantly, is either pushing or being pushed familiar? If so, how? Is pushing something you do as a method of moving through your day? Is being pushed something that you are quite familiar with?

Pull: As in the first exercise, A goes into pull mode. Recall the pull story in this chapter or imagine that you want something from the person across from you. Like a vacuum, pull on them.

Do this for about 15 seconds.

The mindful interface is to notice the impact this action has on you and the other, regardless of the role you play. How familiar is this method in your life? Are you used to pulling or being pulled?

Stop: After finding your baseline, A goes into stop. Shut down. Withhold. Cease any relational flow. Are you breathing? It's hard to be in *stop* and breathe.

Hold stop for 15 seconds.

What is the impact on you and the relationship? Is this a familiar method that you experience through your day or through your life?

Of course, you can mix and match these methods. Trade roles. Hold or express one without telling your partner. See if your partner can name the method. Each partner can embody a different method at the same time.

In the real world of work, social, and family interactions we are always in push, pull, stop, or neutral. Use your journal to record your responses to the following prompts:

- My favorite method is _____.
- I mostly use it with _____.
- I most commonly use it when _____.

- Sometimes I will use _____ to get what I want.
- This is how push, pull, stop, and neutral affect me:
  - ○ Physically _____
  - ○ Emotionally _____
  - ○ Mentally _____
  - ○ Spiritually _____
- I notice push, pull, stop, and neutral affect others in this way: _____.
- I notice push, pull, stop, and neutral are useful in these circumstances: _____.

The Takeaway

Being in relationship is not about the other.

Being in relationship simply gives us the opportunity to practice. Practice love, kindness, forgiveness, patience. Being in relationship offers us the most intimate way we can observe who we are and how our actions impact our material world and the people in it.

19

Coconut

There is sweet water inside a tender coconut.
Who poured the water inside the coconut?
Was it the work of any man?
No. Only the Divine can do such a thing.

—Sri Sathya Sai Baba

My grandson, Ziven, had discovered coconuts during a family trip to the tropics. He was excited as he ran through the kitchen door with a coconut in his hands.

"Look at this, look at this," he said with great animation. His arms waved. His voice was pitched as he headed to the utensil drawer, looking for an instrument to pry open his prize. He knew there was coconut milk inside that stringy brown shell. He was eager to get the sweet liquid.

Happy to help, I directed him to a hammer and a big nail. Ziven focused intently on this task. In a short time, he'd chiseled a hole big enough for some milk to dribble out.

We set the coconut, holes down, in a large glass. The more the glass filled, the more excited Ziven got. Somehow, in this excitement, the glass and the coconut fell over.

No big deal. There was still plenty of fluid remaining.

We cleaned it and this time set it on the floor, thinking that would be more stable than on a wobbly table with a wiggly five-year-old jostling around. But in just a few minutes, that glass also got knocked over. Something about a squirmy kid, a top-heavy glass, and the expectation of sweet coconut milk.

No big deal. We cleaned that up. We shook the coconut to verify that there was still some milk inside. This time, we propped it securely in a pan. We put the pan on the floor in the corner.

Finally, milk — slightly dirty — pooled in the bottom of the pan. Now we were ready to crack the hard shell of the coconut. We gathered everything, and with arms full, headed for the concrete floor out in the walkway.

I don't know what hit the floor first, but I heard clattering and turned to see the pan, the coconut, the towel, and the hammer on the floor. The milk was splattered everywhere. I saw Ziven's disappointment and felt my own frustration. The whole idea was to help Ziven get the milk. That couldn't happen now, and I was irritated that we had lost that experience.

No big deal. We still had the nut with the sweet meat inside. And what five-year-old doesn't want to smash something with a hammer?

After a few hearty bashes, the hard shell gave way. The husk, now split, revealed not the bright white flesh we expected but a discolored, moldy, rotten center.

Ziven looked at it, said yuck, and ran off to play.

But I stood there, paused in thought and action, looking at the open husk with the moldy insides. How interesting, I thought, that because we spilled the milk four times we did not collect enough to drink.

Here is a common dynamic we experience when faced with obstacles: How do we proceed? Do we take the obstacles as dire signals? Question our course of action? Heed these obstacles as warnings and stop our endeavor?

Or are we being tested for our commitment and dedication? Should we forge ahead, persistently working through these obstacles until we reach the intended outcome?

What is the universe communicating to us? And is there a greater life lesson at play?

The universe continuously gives us information, signs, and signals. We all have intuition and insight that influence our life and guide the choices we make. Did the repeated spilling of the coconut milk signal that the nut was spoiled, and we should not proceed? Or was it a test of the due diligence needed to create an outcome by overcoming obstacles?

Every endeavor we embark on will present these two, seemingly opposite, potential interpretations. Certainly, this experience offered universal life lessons on both ends of the spectrum.

A mindful life is a life of curiosity, thoughtfulness, witnessing, and being open to the infinite possibilities of all things known and unknown.

It is easy to look back and say, "The universe sent four clear signals that we should not proceed with drinking the milk."

The key to a mindful life, a curious soul, is to explore with wonderment. How easy it is to get wrapped up in normalcy and to lose sight of the deeper inspiration of the interplay between life and consciousness that infuses each breath we take.

Follow curiosity and obstacles become opportunities.

Follow with passion the due diligence needed to pursue goals and obstacles become doorways.

Frequently, these opportunities and doorways will not lead you to your expected outcome. However, just as frequently, they will open to infinite potential and greater awareness.

That is the mindful life.

As I stood there, paused in thought and action, looking at the open husk with the moldy flesh, I thought, "My irritation and frustration has turned into a great gift if I allow this event to be meaningful enough to enhance my awareness about how I mindfully live my life."

Incarnation is a series of manifest events offered to us by the universe with the intention that our soul departs this life wiser than it entered. The universe offers these events for us all the time, in every day and every breath.

The universal lesson and transformational moment here had nothing to do with a coconut. The transformational moment was not about listening to or ignoring messages from the universe, though it could have been. It was not about diligently forging ahead when obstacles confront us, though it could have been about that also.

This universal lesson had everything to do with the limiting pattern that occurs when things don't turn out the way we want. It was an exquisite opportunity to transform a mundane repetitive pattern that comes into play when events don't unfold the way we expect them to.

Frustration is a common emotion when events don't unfold the way we want them to. There are others: anger, disappointment, withdrawal. What is your favorite emotion?

Frustration arises when we believe things must be or look a particular way for them to be valuable. Demanding that events occur in a particular way is an outcome-oriented, result-oriented pattern. In this pattern, we lose sight of being relational and in the present moment because we are focused on the future. We demand that our experiences have a specific result — in this case, coconut milk.

Due to my frustration, I focused on the outcome. I missed what was occurring in the present moment — in this case, being present with my grandson.

There is nothing inherently wrong or unenlightened about creating outcomes. A mindful life can be full of creative outcomes... or not.

The universe cares less about the outcomes we produce. The universe cares more about how we navigate our life's endeavors.

The Takeaway

The universe, in its patient wisdom, asks, "Who and how do you wish to be when your life experience doesn't line up with your expectations?"

Living a mindful life deepens as we became aware of limiting habitual patterns. With positive intention and courage, we can step back and witness who we are in that pattern. We can catch a glimmer of who the universe is asking us to become.

20

Inspiration: The Breath of Life

We know what we are, but know not what we may be.

—William Shakespeare

BREATHE IN. BREATHE out.

Now be mindful.

Breathe in. Be mindful. Breathe out. Repeat.

Mindfulness, like breathing, is a daily practice. Our lives are full of the essential and mundane details of day-to-day living. Do the laundry. Find socks that match. Sweep the floor. The act of conscious breathing has the ability to infuse the essence of mindfulness into the most mundane details of our lives.

Details can be bothersome and distracting from the mindful life we long to inhabit. "Just let me get through cleaning the bathroom, then I can do my yoga and center myself so I can be more mindful."

But consider that the details of life are the essential manifestations, like a thread or breadcrumbs, they can enhance our Great Quest and direct us on our path.

The universe gives us the small things — these threads, these breadcrumbs — that guide us through our human experience. They inspire us to move always closer to our destination of enlightenment.

When was the last time you felt inspired? What was it that inspired you? Perhaps you heard about a particularly touching act of kindness. Maybe you know of someone who overcame a difficult obstacle to reach a goal. Someone recovered from a trauma to better the lives of others. Perhaps you stood on the precipice, at the edge of the mountain, after a strenuous hike to witness the sun slide below the horizon as the sky turned crimson and azure.

We are all familiar with breathtaking stories, events, and places. These people, stories, and locations can affect us deeply. Being inspired can motivate us to be more proactive and engaged in our life.

When we feel inspired, something deep in the core of our being begins to reverberate. This resonance activates and affirms our capacity to connect with the greatest attributes of what it is to be human. To feel worthy. To feel valuable. To feel an integral part of this dance of life. To feel as though we count and can effect change and bring meaning to our life and the lives of others.

To feel that what we once deemed impossible may now be possible.

High Heart

This resonant inspiration evokes a sense of empathy, compassion, and connection to the spiritual and material worlds and the beings that inhabit both.

This resonance also awakens a place deep within us. It is that place, at the core of our high heart, where our own desire to reach our greatest potential resides. Our high heart is energetically located just above the center of the chest, behind the upper third of our sternum. People frequently put their hands there when speaking of their desires.

Put your hand there. It's about three inches below your collar bones and in the middle of your chest. Energetically and esoterically, our dreams and goals reside here. When we wish upon a star, it is from this place that we connect to the cosmos of infinite possibilities. When we fold our hands to pray, we place them near our high heart.

And be it from shyness or fear of humiliation, it is the place we pull in and cover with rounded shoulders and downcast eyes. It is a place that we often keep hidden and don't acknowledge.

When another person or event inspires us, our high heart activates and evokes the feeling that yes — I, too — can shine like the brightest stars.

I, too, can be great and achieve great things.

Inspire

We often view inspiration as something that comes from external events, transformational experiences, and breathtaking places. The word inspire comes from the Latin "To breathe." In its simplest sense, inspire is the act of inhaling. It is the process of breathing in.

Merriam-Webster defines inspire as "To exert an animating, enlivening, or exalting influence on." Translated first in the early 1600's, the King James Bible reads in Genesis 2:7, "And the LORD God formed man of the dust of the ground and breathed into his nostrils the breath of life; and man became a living soul."

In this context, inspiration literally means "To breathe in and be filled with the spirit of the gods." Inspiration means to be influenced, moved, or guided by the divine or supernatural.

In this moment, take a moment. Relax your belly and inhale gently and fully. In this moment, in the most mundane of all our daily motions, in this most essential of life functions, this breath of life done 15 times a minute, 23,000 times a day, 6 million times from birth to death, is truly an inspirational event.

You are, in this moment and the next moment with this breath and the next breath allowing yourself to "Breathe in and be filled with the spirit of the gods."

You are, in fact, inspiring.

One would think that an activity we do 23,000 times a day would be something we would be very good at. Yet we never stop looking outside for this inspiration. In contrast to being inspired by others and the world around us, what would it be like, in our own way, to consciously inspire ourselves, to look inward — not outward — for our inspiration?

In a mindful life, the transformational question becomes:

- How do I inspire myself?

- How do I exert an animating, enlivening, or exalting influence on my own life?

- How do I find mindfulness and meaning in the simple, yet essentially profound, act of breathing in this precious, endlessly challenging, gift of incarnation?

- In so doing, how do I create moments that can become grand in my life and that allow me to make my life truly inspirational?

All of us are born with certain gifts and natural talents. These gifts that we know and share with the world enrich humanity. They also can be rewarding and satisfying on a personal level. If at age ten we are a virtuoso at the piano or divine the mysteries of the universe by 13, we can be sure that these talents are a carryover from previous lifetimes of honing and practicing certain skills.

But these gifts, in spite of their profound nature, do not constitute our evolutionary edge.

Our evolutionary edge — that which will expand our consciousness, engage us to become more mindful, and transform our lives — is directly correlated to those patterns and experiences in our life that we do not know how to do. For what would be the incarnational point of doing what we already know?

In this classic Catch-22, we are called to inspire ourselves by doing that we habitually would not do. We are called to develop aspects of our self that we have no idea how to develop.

In this world of duality, we have free will and choice. We are not hapless creatures of a divine plan. We are co-creators of our own divine unfolding experiences. We are free to make the choice between our habits and repeating experiences and the significantly more challenging choice of delving into unfamiliar territory. Living a mindful life requires us to embrace life experiences that by choice take us into territory that, because it is unfamiliar, we find discomforting.

This is the territory that our body and mind resist but our soul longs for. This is our evolutionary task.

This is our Great Quest.

But how do we discover that which we do not know how to do?

The unfamiliar territory in which our evolutionary future lies will be recognized by the siren song that pulls us over and over again, interestingly enough, into *familiar* experiences.

In much the same way the moth is innately drawn from the darkness towards the flame, the aspects of our most evolutionary experiences will always include these three hallmarks:

1. The experiences repeat.

2. The experiences are painful.

3. The experience is something we simultaneously long for yet fear.

This third hallmark is perhaps the most revealing. It proposes that we can discover our evolutionary destiny because it holds an element of what we most desire *and* what we most fear or reject.

Experiences Repeat

That is why they become familiar. Every argument I have ever had carries the same hallmarks: I feel misunderstood. I feel frustrated. I feel physically tense. I blame the other. "I can't believe this is happening again," is something I've said to myself throughout my life. My guess is that you have said it also.

A repetitive experience may be at work. It might be with co-workers or your boss. It may be with family or an intimate partner. It could be with a neighbor or the government. In your journal, complete the following prompts:

This is an area of life in which I have a repetitive pattern: _____.

This is the pattern: _____
_____.

The benefit of a repeating experience is that, with a bit of reflection and patience, the experience goes from "Oh no, here I go again" to "Oh, I get it. This repeating experience continues for my benefit. I get many opportunities to practice, to learn, and to grow. Once I change and I become 'enlightened,' this particular experience no longer repeats."

Without mindfulness, the experience becomes just another instance that reinforces habitual behaviors. It then reinforces a limiting belief that allows us to blame the world for our circumstances.

Whenever a life experience repeats, we know that it is to the benefit of our soul. A soul longs to heal through the development of particular aspects of our psyche.

What aspects, you ask?

The aspects we don't know how to bring forth.

Here is something I know how to do: I know how to feel misunderstood. It's familiar. It repeats. It's painful.

Here is another thing I know how to do: I know how to feel frustrated.

But how about feeling patient, curious, or supported?

These attributes — patience, curiosity, and understanding — are aspects of myself that I am learning to bring forth.

In your journal, complete the following prompts:

1. This is what I know how to do, because I do it all the time: _____. Some examples include yelling, turning away, and blaming.

2. This is what my soul longs to experience: _____ _____. For example, connection, patience, or forgiveness.

Experiences are Painful

Pain sharpens our attention and motivates our desire to grow.

When we are in pain, we want to get out of pain. Being misunderstood is painful. Walking around frustrated may be familiar, but it is painful. Though we can always be grateful for the easy, fun, rewarding events in our life, they do not carry the motivational impact that pain affords us.

In your journal, complete the following prompt:

This is a painful dynamic in my life: _____

_____.

We Long for What We Fear

Here are a few examples:

I desire to be understood. But to be understood, I would have to be vulnerable. I would have to open myself and share deeply and fully. I'm not sure I really want to take the risk. It can be scary to be vulnerable. So therefore, I am not vulnerable enough to share what I really feel.

No wonder others don't understand me.

I desire a committed relationship. But then I would have to give up my independence. I always lose my sense of who I am when in an intimate relationship. It's probably best that they never work out in the long run.

Here is what a patient of mine shared:

"The thing I most desire is acceptance; to feel like I am part of a community of people, as though I really belong. But I notice whenever that starts happening and they begin to treat me like I belong there, when they are accepting of me, I begin to antagonize and lash out, mostly subtly, energetically. I really think that I am most afraid of being like them. Then I begin to think that if the group begins to accept me there must be something very wrong with them. I think they are judging me all the time unfavorably, that is why they don't accept me, but I realize that I am judging them all the time and therefore rejecting them. But I really want to be accepted and belong but then I would have to give up a sense of specialness and I don't want to do that. When I open more consciously, I start to see the good in another and I feel less judgment."

This is a common example of our longing for and rejection of acceptance. It reveals the familiar pattern of rejecting others before they reject us.

Inspiration calls on us to develop aspects of our self that we have no idea how to develop. In this story, the territory of acceptance/rejection holds the repetitive pattern that brings pain. Our relationship to acceptance then becomes the crucible for our mindful task, our evolutionary edge, our transformational moment. It begins when we, like this client, become aware that what we most desire is also what we most fear and therefore are most likely to reject.

The mental gymnastics we go through to navigate this dynamic of longing for what we fear is something that, when viewed with consciousness, helps us discover our incarnational evolutionary task.

Practicing Daily Inspiration

Four useful questions to answer in your journal:

1. Is this an experience that repeats?
2. Is it painful?
3. Does it hold both what I desire and what I fear/reject?
4. Does it hold an evolutionary potential?

With each familiar and repetitive experience, I get to practice:

- Doing the opposite of what I automatically do.
- Feeling differently than I usually feel.
- Thinking of life and myself in ways I usually don't.
- Identifying myself beyond my familiar habits.

That Soulful Driven Quest

I stewed about it for days, this phone call hanging over me, occupying far too much space in my brain and thought process. I had been working on a project with a colleague. To my surprise, she called one day and told me she was leaving the venture. Due to timing and busy schedules, we were unable to talk further. I had already reached out a couple times. Things were OK between us, yet there was some unfinished business.

I had the honor of studying with John Upledger, the founder of craniosacral therapy. He had mentioned in a conversation that there was "no disease without conflict." His words floated through my mind.

I felt conflicted. My rational thought process had lots of reasons — all good — not to bother or follow up with my colleague. There was no need to delve into or hash out the details of someone else's choices.

Yet my soulful driven quest for mindfulness kept tugging at my sleeve. My soul, always motivated by the longing to evolve towards enlightenment, wanted a different experience. My mind and my soul were at odds.

Enlightenment has a price. That price is mindfulness — or dedication or surrender to mindfulness. The transformational moment begins as I become curious about my soul's patient tugging. My soul invites me to risk moving from what is familiar to what is uncomfortable.

In this minor, simple, mundane experience of a departing colleague, the universe offered me an evolutionary experience. How can something so boring and routine be an enlightening moment? I am looking for — hoping and praying for — earth-shaking, soul-rattling, mind-boggling events that will usher me into enlightenment, complete with lightning and thunder and divine insights. Surely, I will certainly recognize *that* moment when it comes. Hallelujah!

The most mundane of daily experiences become the breadcrumbs on my path to enlightenment. This is something I strive to remember on a regular basis. Because, should I wait for that moment, I will likely wait for a long time — months, years, even lifetimes.

As I allow curiosity to fuel me, my breath deepens, I become enlivened. I begin to explore the three hallmarks of any evolutionary experience:

1. The experiences repeat.

2. The experiences are painful.

3. In the experiences are something we simultaneously long for and fear.

It repeats. If I had a dollar for every time I was surprised when someone ended a relationship without warning, I could retire to the French Riviera. I do not blame the others. I do not blame myself. And I recognize that there are always numerous — often quite evident — signs leading to any relationship change. Aren't there? I'm just saying I was surprised.

I'm the common denominator in my experiences.

The universe shuffles different players in and out of my life. It changes the characters I deal with. But the pattern and experience remain the same. I'm surprised that someone steps out of the relationship. I am insightfully reflective and patient as I notice this repeating experience.

It's painful. This pattern of repeated, surprising changes in my relationships has been painful.

I want and fear it. I long for authenticity. A sense of comfort within myself that is open-hearted and resilient to changes in life. I fear authenticity. Being authentic means I would have to express what I really thought or felt. I would be vulnerable. That's scary. I would have to be resilient. Then I wouldn't be able to blame the other for how I felt surprised or hurt or disregarded.

The Mundane Supports the Soul's Journey

What am I practicing? First, here is what I already know how to do. Here is how I have identified myself. I am the one who:

- Follows my rational thought process.
- Talks myself out of taking an uncomfortable risk.
- Persuades myself that this (whatever this may be at any given moment in my life) is all much ado about nothing.
- Blames, is frustrated, and feels hurt.

Here is what I get to practice. This is who I *get to be*. I am the one who:

- Follows my heart.
- Takes risks.
- Finds soulful comfort in expressing how I feel and what I think. I am authentic.

Your turn. Take up your journal and respond to the following prompts:

- I already know how to, or I have already identified myself as _____.
- I am the one who

_____

_____

_____

- Here is what I get to practice. This is who I _get to be_. I am the one who:

_____

_____

_____

I am in this moment and the next with this breath and the next. I am inspiring.

The Takeaway

When we hold in our consciousness the soulful truth of who we _get to be_ and who we truly are, our breath deepens. Our inspiration deepens. We are being filled with the spirit of the gods. We are enlivened, we are inspiring.

As we do this, we inspire not only ourselves, but others.

True inspiration happens when we see something in ourselves that we did not imagine we could do, be, or create. It arises in the most mundane aspects of our life. It grants us the opportunity to practice. To inspire.

21

Withholding Love

Being deeply loved by someone gives you strength,
while loving someone deeply gives you courage.

—Lao Tzu

THE SHEETS, DAMP from the heavy salt air, felt cool against my sunburned skin. Happily tired after a full day in the sand and the surf, I lay listening to the symphony of waves. The ocean's rhythmic roar filled the room through the open window next to my bed. I slept easily, kept company by the ever-present grains of sand. My dreams were adrift in the adventurous land where the sea sweeps the beach.

As a kid, I had spent many such days and many such nights and many such summers at my grandparent's home on the Jersey shore.

My grandmother was a first-generation Jew whose family owned a mercantile in the Germantown borough of Philadelphia. Born before the automobile, air travel, or antibiotics she lived through two world wars, the Great Depression, and the loss of a child at birth. Her mother died when she was just nine years old.

By all accounts, my grandmother was a strong woman. She worked hard. She was lively, engaged, present, and loving. She was a straight shooter. We knew when she was happy or upset, busy or relaxing. We certainly knew when she was angry.

She taught me many things: resilience, the attributes of diligence and dedication, showing love through generosity and caretaking. Her laughter knew no limits to the day or the time or the company she was in.

Our parents and grandparents, great-grandparents, and great-great-grandparents bring forward through each generation our ancestral patterns. Patterns are the behaviors and traits that run in families. When we say, "I can't believe I'm acting like my mother" or "He's just like his grandfather," we speak of these ancestral patterns. It could be a look, a walk, a habit, a belief, or a behavior. It could be heart disease or diabetes. It could be how we laugh or what we eat.

In fact, who we are is a direct manifestation of both the nurture and the nature aspects of our family of origin. And, whether or not we pay attention to them, the patterns, traits, and behaviors we carry will pass onto our children.

Ancestral Timelines

Imagine, if you will, a great timeline that stretches behind you. It is a well-trodden path that winds its way back through the ages before eventually fading into the mists of primordial time.

This is the road that your ancestors walked. Through them, their experiences, and their genetics, you also walk it. This is your heritage. This is your past. From the time of your birth to this present moment, you have walked this timeline. And in this incarnation, you are the manifestation of all the paths traveled and all the experiences of your forebears.

In each of our many lives, we walk from the past towards the future though we never leave the present moment. We carry and are carried by our ancestral patterns.

Now imagine this same path stretching out before you. The road ahead is virgin territory. It's what you have yet to create, discover, or experience. Ahead are your offspring, the generations yet to come that will eventually take their place in this ancestral timeline.

This is your future.

You may envision some of the events on the road towards the future, just as you know some of the events of your past heritage.

We are inextricably tied to this timeline. Like a fly in a spider web - our actions, thoughts, and feelings will ripple in both directions along this continuum. Because of this dynamic, the effort we put into mindfulness and transformation effect not only our life, but the lives of those who came before us and the lives of those who will follow in our footsteps.

In transformational work, it is rare that our greatest evolutionary opportunities revolve around the graceful, open, flowing, heartfelt, unifying aspects of our life. In our karmic agreement with the universe, this life will offer us both ease and challenge. Most commonly, our greatest evolutionary rewards arise not from the easy stuff, but the hard stuff. It involves difficulty, pain, and those places in life where we are blocked or struggle.

It was a drafty old farmhouse set deep in the apple orchard. Once the proud home of the landowner, now it was a rental for the farm hands who followed the seasons and worked the crops along the fertile banks of the Columbia River.

I worked those orchards in the earliest years of marriage. I lived in that drafty old farmhouse. I carried into my young adult life my family's ancestral patterns of resilience, of diligence and dedication, and of showing love through generosity and caretaking. These are the grace filled aspects of who I am. They are infused into my genetics and my behavior by my parents and grandparents, great-grandparents and all the generations that walked the path before me.

A mindful life reveres and claims the grace filled aspects of who we are. A transformational life begins to bring awareness to the discordant and painful aspects of who we are. Pain is a remarkable experience. It forces us to pay attention. Part of our soul's evolution demands that we discover an ancestral pattern waiting to be healed.

Awareness, the ability to be responsive, and making a choice for unity rather than separation are touchstones on the road of enlightenment and in living a mindful life.

Discovering an Ancestral Pattern

I can hear my ancestors whispering encouraging words. "You can in this lifetime discover and set aside the burden that this family has carried for eons. And in doing so, you will heal not only your life but the generations that have come before you and those that will follow you."

To begin this discovery, we need to ask:

What is the ancestral burden, passed through the biology and the biography of my forebears, that I now carry infused in my cells?

The inquiry would be to insightfully ask:

What action did I observe or experience in my childhood that evoked pain? How does that behavior or pattern evoke pain now?

Record the answer in your journal:

This is a behavior or pattern that I witnessed or experienced in my childhood that creates pain: _____

_____.

This pain can either be witnessed in our effect on another or felt in our own persona. What you observed as a child and what you do as an adult are usually one and the same. We do what was done to us.

The behavior I observed from my family of origin was a pattern of separation. My grandmother seeded the pattern. It sprouted and grew, like a vine, through our family's behavior. I witnessed it in my mother and my sister. No doubt my grandmother experienced it from her most predominant childhood teachers, parents, and caregivers.

This pattern of separation arises any time there is upset or disagreement. My family uses it to show displeasure or hurt. Though it may take on many masks in its presentation, at its core, it is the well-honed and much practiced pattern of withholding love.

I was so well schooled in this method of showing my disapproval, this ability to withhold love, that I carried it — like an old scar, familiar and forgotten — unknowingly and (in hindsight) pervasively into young adulthood and my marriage.

Triggered by a disagreement, a perceived disregard, a conversation that devolved into a loud and heated argument, I could — with ease — shut down and stop any contact, conversation, or flow of love. I could do this for hours, even days. My goal was to show the other just how wrong they were and to punish them by withholding myself, my attention, and my love.

I believed that if I did this, the other would eventually understand and change their behaviors. I did this not from any mindful or enlightened place. I did this because it's what I learned to do from my genetics and my childhood environment.

How familiar is it for you to withhold your love? To shut down your own energy, hold a tight constraint in your chest, and compress your breath? Is there a demand that you place on the other — that is, what they need to do, how they need to act or be — before you will allow your love to be expressed? If this is something you're familiar with, I ask you with compassionate curiosity:

Who is it you are punishing when you withhold your love?

When we were young and without the tools and experience of an adult body and adult consciousness, there was a limit to how we could or believe we could control our environment. Our entire world may have been the sphere of our crib, bedroom, mother, father, siblings.

As a baby, we would have noticed — even at this very early developing stage of consciousness — that if we were able to restrict that flow of energy through our body, we would exert some effect. We would exert such an effect on our own internal domain, and likely would have noticed an effect on our external environment. What if — in that withholding of breath, feeling, or flow of energy — we received a response from the environment? Someone noticed. A change occurred.

Consider how powerful that would feel to a child.

With child consciousness, it is important to remember that any such response — good or bad, healthy or unhealthy — feels empowering. Therefore, it would become a lifelong foundational pattern for how to interface with our own body and the world around us.

In addition, we observe behavioral patterns in our primary and most cellularly influential teacher, our parents. It's easy to imagine a situation when, as a young child, we witnessed our mother, perhaps upset at our father, withhold her love, attention, and energy. That is, we likely witnessed our mother withhold her full capacity to be in full relationship with our father.

If this modeling by our parents was prevalent in our environment, we would have learned this behavioral pattern even if we were at a preverbal or perambulatory age. We would have learned this behavior because our brain wave patterns, neural development, and energetic field development at that age create a situation in which we are fully open to all influences from our environment.

As a child with exceptionally impressionable consciousness, we discovered ways to interact with our world that enabled us to have a sense of control. We developed a set of tools, mostly from the modeling of our parents, that enabled us to survive. That's how we began to create a sense of self that is interactive with our environment.

Though this is an essential element of our development, there is a limitation to this pattern. The limitation is that, as we grow up and develop mentally, physically, and especially emotionally, it becomes exceedingly difficult to shed these patterns that were hardwired into that very impressionable consciousness when we were so young.

As children we have a developing body: brains, cells, nervous system, and an emotional field that functions pretty much like a recording device. We have all been reminded of this by a child who repeats or reacts to an adult conversation the adult thought was private or too sophisticated for the child to hear or comprehend.

Not until the development of discretion, around age seven, can a child begin to make choices about what comes into their psyche and what doesn't. This age correlates to our brain-wave patterns changing from a predominance of Theta and Delta waves to a more mature mix with Beta and Alpha waves.

It also correlates to the formation in our energetic field of the screens that protect our chakra, allowing us to filter the overwhelming array of influences from our day-to-day environment.

And it correlates to neural development in the brain, where particular neural pathways become dominant. This reflects and results in habitual patterns of behavior.

These childhood influences, infused into our being, will run our adult behavior until grace, awareness, and conscious choice changes our patterns.

In this example, the habit of withholding love can be seen in muscle tension, shutting down our breath, and decreasing the flow of energy through our heart. Over time, it becomes a firmly embedded dynamic. We then use this pattern consciously — or, more commonly, subconsciously — as a tool to control, communicate, and influence our environment.

Just as we did when we were young.

The Transformational Moment

The transformational moment occurs when we first begin to observe when, where, and how we use this pattern. Any time we withhold our full presence — any time we shut down, withhold our love, get tense, or hold our breath to transmit or show another how we feel — this pattern is at play.

This is a kinesthetic experience. By paying attention, we can feel it in our physical body. We will actually feel this in our chest and in our heart.

The heart, of course, is associated with love. More comprehensively, the heart is associated with our capacity for human connection and relationship.

Due to conflict, strife, disappointment, hurt, or misunderstanding, we drop into child consciousness. Out of habit, we reach into our set of tools. We pull out the pattern that we remember from witnessing our family. We recall how effective and empowering it was to withhold and shut down our energy.

The belief system that underpins this habit is that we can influence those in our environment and communicate how hurt or disappointed we are. The goal is to punish or hurt another by withholding our full creative, loving self. We believe that by transmitting our disappointment in this way it will affect our environment, just as it did in our childhood.

Practice:

In your journal, respond to the following prompts:

It is under these circumstances that I shut down or withhold my love: _____.

I am justified in withholding my love because: _____.

This is how it feels in my body to withhold love:

_____.

Anyone familiar with this pattern of withholding love (that is, everyone) can see how it is a contributing factor in the development of heart disease, the primary cause of mortality in the United States. Energetically, health is a function of balance and flow. The universal life force — qi, prana, vitality, or spirit — is the etheric energy that enlivens our physical body as well as our emotional and mental bodies.

Any time we withhold love, we directly decrease or stop the energy that flows through the heart and the heart chakra. As this happens, we begin to damage the physical function of the heart muscle. Our ability to give and receive love, the main energetic function of the heart chakra, becomes increasingly impaired.

This creates a snowball effect within our physical, mental, and emotional bodies and an ingrained habitual pattern develops.

As we do this again, consciously or subconsciously, we model it for our children. They learn to do it. It becomes the norm in our family. It becomes the norm in our community. It becomes the norm in our culture.

The goal of mindful living and transformational work is not to vanquish these patterns. The goal of mindful living and transformational work is to actively respond to our environment so we can consciously choose which, if any, of the many patterns in our toolbox we wish to employ at any moment.

Unwinding this pattern, or any pattern, begins by recognizing when it is in play. The physical body becomes the instrument that can track this. As we've detailed throughout this experience, physical sensations occur in the body. The chest becomes tight, or there is a shutting down sensation, or even a sense of numbness. If we pay attention, we will recognize the pattern as one that has been used in our family of origin going back through the generations. As we pay attention to this pattern, we will feel separated from whoever we are in relationship with. And here is a key point:

We will feel justified in our behavior to withhold our love.

These are the hallmarks of a limiting pattern: separation and justification.

Unwinding this pattern begins when we breathe into our heart and allow the tension in our body to dissipate. To go deeper, we need to look at the demand we project onto the other. What are we demanding that they need to do or be?

My ability to love is not dependent on your ability to respond.

The capacity to love fully, without holding back, is inherent in the heart of every one of us. When we risk allowing this love to move through our heart, we notice a sensation significantly more pleasurable then withholding. We notice that, though we influence others when we withhold our love, we influence them even more profoundly when we open our heart.

We inflict pain when we punish others by withholding our love. That pain is felt by others, but we feel it most intensely in the center of our own heart. Similarly, others feel the love that flows through our heart, but we experience the pleasure most intensely in our own heart.

A mindful life is a life of conscious choices made from a deepening awareness of who and how we are in the world. Can we make a conscious choice to forgo the habitual discomfort of withholding love and experience the free flow of freedom to love?

Healing this personal, ancestral, and cultural pattern can be enhanced with the embodiment that transmits this message: My ability to love is not dependent on someone else's ability to receive it.

The Takeaway

My ability to love is not dependent on someone else's ability to receive it.

22

Karma

The line it is drawn, the curse it is cast.

—Bob Dylan

"My mother had polio," she said, her voice rueful and resigned.

A slow exhale revealed that her experience had been long-suffering. "It was her karma," she continued. Followed by the question that always hovers around the topic of karma. "I wonder what she did in her previous life to warrant such a painful experience in this life?"

Her mother, who had passed on, appeared as an image in my mind. This commonly happens to me with people who have passed over. Their soul appears, identified by their recent physical attributes. A stream of consciousness appears as well. The consciousness that presents has broken free of the dualistic paradigms of the physical world. The consciousness is always etheric, heavenly, loving, and all-knowing, communicative, nonjudgmental.

I was struck by the sadness carried by this vision of her mother. It was not sadness due to her life with polio and the effect it had on her family and her daughter. It was sadness due to her daughter's misunderstanding about karma. Sadness due to her daughter's misinterpretation that a life with polio was a life of punishment correlated to some past misdeed.

Karma, as a word and concept, has become ubiquitous in American society. The idiom "you reap what you sow" is seen from pop psychology to venerable yogis. When something bad happens to us, we wonder what we did wrong — in this life or another — to deserve such a fate. When life experiences are overwhelming or devastating, we ponder what horrible seeds we must have sown that now makes us reap such a bitter harvest.

When hurt by another, we commonly use karma to justify our thoughts of revenge. We hope, or say, "With karma they will, at some point, get their just rewards."

Yet karma is significantly more then something that we did bad or wrong, in this life or another. It is more than believing, "You reap what you sow." It is more than the lessons we think we need to learn. And it is certainly more than figuring out what we need to do to prevent, release, or relinquish the pain in our life.

Karma is about the evolution of our soul. It is about evolving through the Wheel of 84. The Wheel of 84 refers to the number of created beings or species (84 lakhs or 8.4 million) on this planet. The species are plants, creatures of the land, sea, and sky, human beings, divas. Humans are the pinnacle of the evolutionary procession. By traveling the Wheel of 84, our soul eventually becomes human. As a human, it will spend any number of lifetimes before we attain spiritual enlightenment.

A human birth is the most sacred of all the 84 lakhs.

Karma is about an incarnating soul choosing to have particular experiences in this physical world. These are experiences we dualistically judge as good or bad. Experiences we categorize as either punishments or rewards.

In our quest for a mindful life, we strive to strip away the judgment of good or bad. Instead of categorizing experiences as punishment or reward, we consider them opportunities for the advancement of our soul's development.

Consider karma as synonymous with habit. Over lifetimes, we create habitual patterns. These patterns show up in how we think, how we feel, and how we act. Everything from the way we walk to our dynamics in relationship carries the stamp and flavor of habitual patterns. In our present life, all our habits garnered from this and previous lives — that is, our karma — are in play.

Karma is the choice of particular life experiences that our soul makes prior to incarnation. It is about the brightest of souls diving deeply into the unknown dark duality of life in the physical world.

Karma is the habits and repetitive patterns carried from lifetime to lifetime. We carry these habits and patterns from one life to the next because we have yet to evolve beyond the lesson that these patterns keep presenting to us. Once we grok that lesson, we no longer have the repetitive experience because we dissolve that aspect of our karma. At that point, a piece of the puzzle falls into place. The Wheel of 84 turns a cog. The pattern shifts.

A consciously engaged mindful life is one of witnessing ourselves in our patterns. A mindful life does not use karma as an excuse or retribution.

Karma is not about the past. It is about the present moment. It's about our current life because this is the life we are in. This is the life we can engage with. If it is karmic, and it happened in a past life, it is also happening in this life. If you experienced betrayal in a past life and it has not been resolved, you will experience betrayal in this life.

Don't worry about a past life, there are ample lessons to work on in this life. That is why we have this life.

Dissolving the bonds of karma is about making choices in this life. We have the choice to move beyond our habits.

Karma is about lessons, but it is not what you need to learn. The lessons to learn have to do with the big picture of our life. Karma is about the evolution of the soul. The details of our life are only agreed on experiences that, if witnessed with mindfulness, present us with a way to turn the Wheel of 84 to shift our patterns. These details are usually simple, mundane aspects of our daily life. They continuously offer us practical keys to shift our patterns.

Are you habitually impatient while standing in line at the bank? This experience will continue to happen until you learn the lesson of patience. Once you learn patience, you will no longer find yourself standing impatiently in line at the bank.

That's the big picture: patience. That's the piece of the puzzle that, when it falls into place, shifts our karma.

The line at the bank is a detail. It is only a lesson presented and an opportunity experienced, endlessly, until we no longer need it.

Once we have achieved patience, we no longer have experiences in which we are impatient.

If we want to dissolve karma, we need to make new choices. Dissolving karma is about the most mundane aspects of our present life that always — *always* — center on being kind to ourselves and to others. Those mundane aspects always center on opening our heart to ourselves and to others. Fail to be kind, fail to open your heart, and nothing else you strive to learn or figure out about karma matters.

It's About Courage

Instead of seeing our life experiences, painful or pleasurable, as payback for some good or bad deed, look at karma from the soul's point of view.

We incarnate into a world of duality that has the highest human attributes — love and pleasure — and the lowest human attributes — hate and pain. Imagine your soul, prior to incarnation, standing on the precipice of infinite choice, looking into the vast ocean of incarnational options: rich or poor, fat or skinny, petty or gracious, any of 10,000 options for a single life in this particular incarnation. Then, via free will, our soul signs up for the very life we, in this very moment, are having.

It takes a great deal of courage to dive into that ocean.

To choose a life that encompasses harshness, pain, strife, or struggle is not a life that reflects punishment. It is a life that reflects courage.

Incarnation is done for a purpose. That purpose is not punishment. The idea of punishment is a dualistic concept.

Karma is our soul making clear, courageous, and conscious decisions to have life experiences that give us the maximum opportunities to evolve.

Look at those among us who carry the most earthly burdens. You will see the most courageous soul — a soul that surrendered to the crucible of life in duality to temper itself. Look into the eyes of someone who habitually struggles, and you will see the bravest of souls. The downtrodden. The neglected. Those who live with strife and famine.

Pity not their souls but honor their courage.

Our Greatest Life Task

I consulted with a patient. We discussed spiritual life tasks; commonly known as the reason we are incarnated. "To love myself" was his assessment of his greatest life task.

Our greatest life task is reflected in our greatest longings.

And our greatest longings reflect an aspect of our life that we have yet to manifest.

This un-manifest aspect reflects the places in our life where we struggle the most. We do not long for something we have already created. For this patient, "to love myself" remained an eternal mystery. It was his elusive white whale. It was his greatest struggle, a fifty-four-year struggle through the successes and failures every life holds. His present life strapped him financially. He worked part-time in a hardware store. It was a decent opportunity, but not his deepest longing for a career path. He judged his abilities, his station, and his skills. He felt a failure.

How could he love himself when his life sucked?

Yet from a soul point of view, his current position was the most perfect of all experiences to be had, and not an unfamiliar one. Perhaps the details of working in the hardware store environment were new, but the big picture and the big picture lesson were a repetitive theme.

If you want to learn to love yourself and that is one of your karmic lessons, then create a life situation in which loving yourself would be difficult.

If it were easy, you would have already done it and moved onto another lesson.

To love ourselves when we judge our life a failure is a grand evolutionary task. It is an evolutionary task on the soul level. Would a soul strive for anything less? Here is this experience. Can you love yourself?

Here is a situation where the habit of judgment and self-disdain grows deep. Can you love yourself now?

Here you see yourself as a failure. Can you love yourself now?

It is in such an environment that learning to love oneself and defer judgment takes the greatest courage. Should, in this most challenging dynamic, a glimmer of self-love and kindness arise from the longing of the soul, then karma begins to dissolve. A piece of the puzzle falls into place. The Wheel of 84 turns a cog. A life pattern shifts.

I shared with my patient, whose mother had polio, the image and stream of consciousness I experienced. As I did so, a karmic pattern shifted. Mother and daughter had shared a life of sadness and misunderstanding. Perhaps they had shared several lifetimes. And yet their relationship changed that day. It changed from one of sadness, sorrow, and pain to one of respect, honor, and gratitude for the life chosen and the profound courage it took to do so.

I was at a workshop in San Francisco. My hotel was three or four blocks from the convention center where the seminar was held. After a long day of classes I was hungry and ready to get to my room. I ordered takeout at the corner café and headed for my hotel. This part of San Francisco had its fair share of panhandlers and I spent my walk head down, bag of food clenched to my side, moving briskly to sidestep the vagrants. Still hungry when I arrived at my hotel, I now felt rushed, tense, and irritated.

Though embarrassed to admit it, this was not an isolated pattern of behavior. Looking back on this and other similar circumstances, I can say that this behavior was not a new choice. It did not fall into the category of kindness. My tense body and chest reflected a closed heart, not an open heart.

I was in Florida teaching. Out for a walk, I meandered through the downtown streets on a balmy spring day. I was approached by a mid-50's man with unkempt hair, disheveled clothes, and sockless feet in worn out shoes. He stopped. I stopped. I reached into my pocket. Gathering all my change, I handed him 73 cents.

I am certain that had I handed him the keys to a new car, his reaction could not have been more grateful, gracious, and bless-laden. That, for me, was a new choice. It revolved around kindness. My heart felt open.

The Takeaway

On this long and winding journey home, I am learning.

Awareness is a steppingstone on the path, not an endpoint.

Mindfulness is a practice of patience for ourselves and a practice of kindness for others.

23

The Buster Life

All his life he tried to be a good person.
Many times, however, he failed.
For after all, he was only human. He wasn't a dog.

—Charles M. Schulz

IT'S BEEN SAID that human beings are at the top of the evolutionary ladder. We humans declare ourselves the most evolved of all the species.

Yet I have learned a valuable lesson from one of the so-called lower species. This lesson is worth sharing.

My dog's name was Buster, and as dogs tend to do, he became one of my best friends. In human years, he lived to 94. In dog years, 12. In my heart, he lives forever.

My experience with Buster makes me question which species is most evolved.

Buster lived a good life. He saw every day as a day full of adventure, whether chasing coyotes or laying in the tall grass under the sun. If I saw every day more as an adventure, and less as a list of chores, I could say, "I live a good life."

Buster was there for me every day. Regardless of where I'd been or how long I'd been gone, when I came home, he showed up. Regardless of how I felt, he was happy to be with me. He taught me that the simple act of showing up lets others know just how much we care.

Buster lived in the moment. A few months prior to his death, he was doing so poorly we called the vet so she could come euthanize him. When the vet drove up, he went out to meet her, sniffing and wagging his tail. He was thrilled to have company come by to visit. He certainly was not worried about what was to come next. As it turned out, that wasn't his day to die. He lived well for a couple more months. I can only pray that when I go out to face my own death, I do so with such curiosity and with such in the moment presence.

Buster held unconditional love every moment. Sometimes, when I'm having a really good day, I can hold unconditional love for a few hours. For him, unconditional love was as natural as digging for gophers or barking at the neighbor's horse. Unconditional love, on a cellular level, 24/7. If that were a skill required by the universe to ascend to heaven, how many of us would pass through the pearly gates?

The Takeaway

Human beings may be on the top of the evolutionary ladder, but my experience of The Buster Life – a life full of adventure, of showing up, of being present, and of living in unconditional love, is something I think all of us could strive for.

24

How Do I Wish to Live This Moment?

Between stimulus and response, there is a space.
In that space is our power to choose our response.
In our response lies our growth and our freedom.

—Viktor E. Frankl

THERE IS A common paradigm in New Age thinking that goes something like this:

For me to be enlightened and live a mindful life, I need to acknowledge that I am responsible for what happens to me.

This concept carries a hidden implication that can become quite harmful and often hurtful. It occurs when we conflate the notion of responsibility with the notion of blame. It then goes something like this:

"I am to blame for my situation."

Which morphs easily into, "I must have done something wrong.

Or, more simply, "I must be bad."

I see this commonly enough in my practice, especially from patients who are proactively engaged in their health care and their lives. One patient comes to mind.

She is a consciously engaged, young mother of two. She works as a mental health counselor with children's services. She is active in her community, her faith, and her family. Her diagnosis was cancer. She came to my office wondering what she did wrong. Certainly, she must have done something wrong to deserve such a fate.

This patient, in all her pure intentions and conscious efforts to mindfully live her life, had translated the "I am responsible for my situation" paradigm into "I am to blame for my situation".

Foundationally, taking responsibility is an essential part of the moral fiber that weaves through our individual lives and the fabric of our society. To conscientiously and independently lay claim to one's actions is both empowering and inspiring. Being responsible is not always the easiest action to take. But the more we take that action, the more courageous we become.

Being courageous is foundational in our quest to live a mindful life.

However, there is a distinction to be made between being responsible and being responsive. Being responsible for life experiences is not the same as being responsive to life experiences.

One of the most powerful ways we can define responsibility is by breaking the word into *response* and *ability*. Or more precisely, defining response-ability as *having the ability to respond*.

This definition relieves the burden we place on ourselves.

It lifts the blame of, "I must have done something wrong — otherwise, this wouldn't be happening to me." My patient did nothing wrong. She is not responsible for her cancer. The guilt this New Age paradigm bestows does not enhance her healing, it does not empower her.

She does, through this experience, have the opportunity to respond to her situation. In her response, she moves from being a victim to being empowered.

This, then, becomes both transformational and healing.

When I was in naturopathic medical school, I had the opportunity to preceptor with Dr. Melvin Morse. A preeminent Seattle pediatrician, Dr. Morse wrote the bestselling book *Closer to the Light*. After a full day of ear infections, newborns with jaundice, rotavirus, and the sporadic rash, we headed to the hospital to do some rounds. I threw my backpack in his car and off we went.

The hospital was quiet. We followed up with a few patients we had seen earlier that day. Then we debriefed the salient points of pediatric care from both the mechanistic model of modern medicine and the comprehensive model of alternative medicine. We came to the agreement that, though we approach medicine from different platforms, our intents and goals aligned: caring for others.

With the hour getting late, it was soon time for me to go. I needed to get my backpack from Dr. Morse's car. As he handed me the keys, he told me to toss them under the seat as he had to finish up a few things before he could leave.

I walked to the car in the cool, damp Seattle night. I grabbed my backpack. I tossed the keys under the seat. Then, dutifully, habitually, and mechanically, I locked the car door.

The instant the door slammed shut, I knew what I had done. I stood there, in denial and disbelief, for several moments. I tried opening the door more than a few times. I pawed my fingers along the window. I checked under the fenders for a hidden key. Every attempt to resolve the reality before me proved futile.

With mild panic setting in, various options ran through my mind. I could walk away, get in my pickup, and find my way home through the drizzle. This would, at some point, require me not to fess up, but to say, "What? The car was locked? Are you kidding?" I'd need to come up with some such shocked response to deflect the responsibility of my actions.

This scenario was both immediately appealing and deeply tainted by the long reach of the father-son relationship I had in childhood. In psychology it's called transference. Transference is when we experience the present situation through the veils of the past, so we react as though the past event were occurring now. Had this event occurred with my father, I would have had a tsunami of anger and frustration crashing into my delicate and young child psyche.

This body-mind memory and cellular reaction was activated the moment that car door clicked shut.

No wonder the fight, flight, or freeze reaction was my primary choice.

The universe, it seems, presents the most mundane experiences to further our soul's most profound evolutionary potential. Keys locked in a car. You really can't get any more mundane than that.

The universe only wants to know, "How, Steve Stroud, do you respond?"

Or the universe could also ask:

- If I were to hold self-evident the ideal manifestation of my incarnation, who in this moment would I be?

- Who and what kind of being could I be?

- Who and what kind of person do I get to be?

- What kind of human being do I wish to convey — not to others, for their approval or appeasement, but to myself?

I began to define myself as a person who walks the earth with a clear and unified intention of developing a sense of self that reflects a conscious choice of my greatest potential in that evolutionary space between stimulus (slamming the car door) and response.

How do I get to live this moment?

Who do I *get* to be?

There I stood, in the ever-dampening air, peering into the locked car. Peering into the space between reality and denial. Suspended between my cellular transference and my beckoning evolutionary potential.

My choice was not to walk to my pickup. I made the choice not to practice my habitual impulse to deny responsibility.

Instead, I listened to a deeper calling. I walked towards the hospital door and my unfolding future.

What I could not know at the time is that this transformational experience would allow me, years later, to support my young patient with their daunting cancer diagnosis.

It allowed me to ask her, "How do you wish to live this moment?"

She began to allow the feelings of forgiveness and kindness to soothe her worried soul. Because that is how she wanted to live. She wanted to live with faith, not with fear and remorse.

She began to untether the chains of blame and guilt that imprisoned her life force.

She began to challenge a culturally pervasive paradigm that said, "Because you are responsible for your fate, you must have done something wrong to deserve it."

She lifted the burden of blame for her situation.

This enabled and empowered her to respond to her situation. This became the foundation for her healing and her transformation.

Practice:

If you were to ask yourself, "How do I wish to live this moment? Who do I *get* to be?" once in your journey through life, your guiding angels would take notice. Previously unseen guideposts on your road to enlightenment would begin to appear.

If you were to ask yourself, "How do I wish to live this moment? Who do I *get* to be?" at any life juncture where you faced strife or moral quandary, your guiding angels would smile and toast champagne.

If you were to ask yourself, "How do I wish to live this moment? Who do I *get* to be?" throughout your day, your angels would show up in your life wearing the garb of love, compassion, kindness, and forgiveness.

When you no longer ask yourself, "How do I wish to live this moment? Who do I *get* to be?" because you have embodied both the question and the higher-self answer, your Great Quest will be nourished and sustained by the angelic tears of joy that fall from the heavens.

The Takeaway

The practice is to ask yourself, "How do I wish to live this moment? Who do I *get* to be?"

25

This is Who I Get to Be

Try not to become a man of success, but
rather try to become a man of value.

—Albert Einstein

THIS WAS MY senior year. Classes in the morning, a part-time job in the afternoon, clinic shifts in the evening. A vision of life beyond medical school would sporadically appear, only to evaporate into the reality of the schedules, shifts, tasks, and exams.

Today, like so many other days, I was at the end of my rotation. It was late, I was tired, and I was hungry. Seattle in the winter is cold and dark and misty wet. I finished my charting and quickly gathered my gear and books. I was intent on catching that next bus home.

As I headed for the door, a classmate asked if I wanted a ride. I was elated. The thought of a warm vehicle sure beat the prospect of standing in the elements waiting for the metro. I said sure and we headed out into the damp night.

What We Have

In our culture, it is common to link our self-worth with money and our material possessions. As in, the more money I have - the more value I have.

There is, of course, truth to this.

A professional sports player who makes $10 million more than his teammates is seen as having greater value than the other players. There is nothing particularly wrong with using money as an identifier of value, so long as it is not our sole identifier.

Throughout our life, material things may come or go based on many factors — family, education, health, unforeseen events, and the choices and opportunities both taken and abandoned.

Regardless of our socio-economic position, it's important to remember that in the context of our soulful evolution, **the universe is more interested in the relationship we develop with our possessions than in the total accumulation of them.**

As we strive for a mindful life, it is useful to acknowledge the extent to which we equate our money and possessions with our self-worth. We all do it to some extent. What's useful in our Great Quest is to be honest with ourselves about that extent.

Money and mindfulness are not mutually exclusive.

Nor does a monastic life, in thought or deed, equate to being more enlightened.

It's not how much or how little we have — it's our *relationship* to how much or how little we have.

We incarnate into the material world rife with temptation and desire; we are much like the proverbial kid in the candy store. In this incarnation, the evolutionary question of self-worth becomes:

Can we stay embodied in our spiritual nature among the temptations of the material world?

Practice

Part of how we identify ourselves is through what we have. Take a few moments with your journal to inventory the things you possess that reflect your value. As you do this, remember it is neither good nor bad to have material things.

For example, consider your home:

This is my home's value: _____

This is how my home defines who I am: _____

_____.

Other material and non-material possessions in your valuation could include cars, your job, your family, or art and jewelry, tools or clothes.

As you compile this inventory and assign values to it, you'll probably grow even more acutely aware that our culture equates self-worth with, and defines it by, our possessions.

That's OK.

Because the question isn't how much you have or how much it's worth. The question of this exercise becomes:

Can we go beyond our culture's definition to develop a broader sense of self?

Should we fall into the belief that our value as a person is based solely on the equation $\$ = me$ or $I = \$$, then the common cultural paradigm of linking money to our sense of self can become an obstacle in our quest for mindfulness.

Drive a Rolls-Royce or a Ford Pinto. Live in a castle or in the projects. The universe will ask only this:

Is the Rolls-Royce your identity, or is it just a car?

That is, do you desire a Rolls-Royce, a mansion, a rare artifact, or another material thing just so you can feel OK about yourself?

One of the greatest gifts that deep personal transformational work affords us is the opportunity to broaden how we define ourselves.

My elation at catching a direct ride home in a warm car soon gave way to a fidgety sense of angst. I was a strapped medical student living in a crackerjack house with my wife and kids. The $365 a month mortgage was always paid, but often late. What would my classmate think if he saw the place? What would he think of me?

"Thanks," I said. "You can drop me off. I can walk from here. No sense in going out of your way. The corner here is fine, my house is just a block away…."

I was embarrassed. I was afraid that my classmate would define me and judge me because I lived in a rundown neighborhood in a ramshackle house.

My internal sense of worth was not strong enough to honor my current station in life. I could not value the hard work and dedication it took just to achieve what I had. I fell into the common cultural dynamic of linking my possessions with my self-worth.

I was fortunate, as we all are, that the patient universe would give me many more opportunities to discover and to broaden my sense of self.

What We Can Do

What we have is one way we define our self-worth.

A broader definition of self-worth includes what we can do.

Imagine you are traveling in a foreign country and you lose your cash, your passport, and your credit card. Fortunately, in this scenario, you can do something that is of great value. You can speak the local language.

This is a simple example of how we broaden our sense of self-worth from *what we have* to *what we can do*. Manifesting our skills and our creativity is another way that we express our value.

Our sense of well-being and contentment in life correlates to the extent we are able to express our creativity. Manifesting what we can do fuels our sense of self-worth because it ignites our life force. Various cultures know this life force as prana, qi, vitality, spirit, or energy.

This life-affirming current nourishes and sustains our body and soul. This vital energy may look big or may look small. That makes no difference. It is the expression that counts. I speak a foreign language, I bake cookies for the senior center, I can paint a landscape or fix a leaky sink.

Practice:

In your journal list the ways you express your creative energies.

This is what I do that is creative: _____, _____, _____.

This is what I do that enhances my sense of self-worth or value: _____, _____, _____ _____.

As *what we can do* manifests into the material world, two dynamics occur that cultivate our self-worth. One is an expressive aspect. The other is a reflective aspect.

Expression

As we express what we can do — be it sing or change the oil in our car — we release our creative life force. The expression of this life force nurtures our sense of self.

In the manifestation of our creativity, a current of self-worth flows through our body and soul. You can feel this energetic flow through sensations on a physical level as well as on an emotional level. For example, when you finish a task that requires a creative effort, you might feel a release of tension, a deepening of breath, a delightful exhilaration, or a more solid sense of self. On an emotional level you might feel elated, joyful, or satisfied.

In your journal, express how you feel physically and emotionally when you are creative: _____ _____.

Reflection

When this creative life force, this *what we can do*, is manifest into the material world, we will get a reflection back. Others will give us their opinion of our efforts.

Here is where vulnerability and courage come into play. Here is where the rubber meets the road in our quest for living a mindful life.

Imagine a crab along the ocean's edge, skittering from sand to rock to crevice. At some point, for this crab to grow, it must shed its protective shell. Yet without its shell there is little to protect its tender flesh from the harsh elements. To go beyond its own limitations, this crab must endure periods of great vulnerability.

We are no different than this sea-dwelling crustacean. Growth requires vulnerability. Vulnerability requires courage.

Have you ever gotten a standing ovation, received an award, been paid for your work, or been told, "Nicely done"?

That's a reflection. That's the opinion of others supporting your creative endeavors.

Have you ever bombed? Have you ever been rejected, turned down, or fired? That also is a reflection. That is also the opinion of others supporting your creative endeavors — although doing so in the way your ego might not like.

Our soulful evolution and our discovery of value must go beyond what we like and don't like. When we are vulnerable enough to express our creative efforts, we demonstrate the essential quality of courage.

The expression of what I can do is more than a list of accomplishments. A useful metaphor is the opening of a flower.

The flower opens not for the approval of others, but for the pure expression of what it is to be a flower.

It is in this simple act the flower owns its value.

As we affect others with our act of doing, we become that flower. It is through our presence and our human connection — through the pure expression of what it is to be who we are — that we bring immeasurable value to the world.

When we think about what we can do, we usually think about physical tasks. Yet there is something we can do that transcends the material. It is a simple act that confirms our value and the value of others. It is this:

We can love.

Take a breath. Bring yourself present.

I can love.

Repeat a few times.

Is there a greater sharing of the human spirit — of our prana, our energy, our qi — than being able to love?

I can love.

I can love in the face of pain or conflict. I can love in those circumstances when it would be easier (or more habitual) to shut down my heart. I can live mindfully, compassionately, and patiently.

As we bring forward this amazing thing we can do, we begin to fully embody and understand the depth of our value as human beings.

When you feel there is nothing else you can do, there is always — *always* — one more thing you can do.

You can love.

Who We Are

It was the ides of March in the year 1975. An otherwise unremarkable day in an unremarkable week except that I was standing, not without design, in a small dusty pull-out on Route 1 just south of the DC beltway. I claimed as my worldly possessions one sleeping bag, a change of clothes, a water bottle, a packet of granola, a pocketknife, and twenty-five dollars.

I wish I could say, for the sake of prose, that there was some great story or drama that placed me on that highway heading south — a broken home, drugs, neglect, or some trauma that drove me to escape into the world at the age of 19.

Alas, it was none of those things.

Ignited by Jack Kerouac's *On the Road*, I desired an experience of life outside the comfort of my middle-class youth.

I wanted to know what it was like to go hungry, to be on my own, and to sleep in the damp weeds and under bridges along the back roads of America. I wanted to eat red beans and rice at Buster Holmes in New Orleans and see the Mojave night sky. I wanted to make my mark, not on the world, but on my own sense of self.

This was something I had to do.

It was one of those few times in life when the universe first whispers, then persuades, then kicks us into action. Driven almost desperately by a desire to prove myself to myself, I found myself standing patiently alongside the highway. A highway that came from the familiar and disappeared into the unknown. Pushed by a rush of air from the big rigs, I kicked at the gravel, took a deep breath, and stuck out my thumb.

Though each of us has a unique incarnational journey, there are common territories of experience that all humans traverse. These include our experiences with relationships, children, work, family, health, and society. The territory of money, value — or more deeply, our self-worth — is essential terrain that we all travel in our artful journey towards mindfulness.

What we have or what we can do are excellent indicators of value. Yet there is one more aspect that needs to be brought forth. This goes beyond having or doing, and though it has to do with our own definition of being, it goes beyond even that.

I have gone to workshops and retreats, traveled miles to study with the masters, placed myself in therapy, in the halls of academia and on the streets of hard knocks. I have explored the reaches of my own deep, dark forests. There are periods in my life when I have been driven by curiosity; other times, I have been washed ashore after the storm of personal turmoil.

Like you, I am a seeker.

Answering the call of our Great Quest.

The life set before us is our soul's journey. From our first inspiration to our last exhalation, it is a voyage swelled by the winds of all that is possible and buffeted by the storms of that which is probable.

We are cast into this adventure not so much to discover the meaning of life, but to uncover, with awareness, those experiences which make our life meaningful.

This journey into this unknown life affords us the freedom of choice, or free will, to experience that which is probable *and* to strive for that which is possible.

Our Great Quest is to broaden our sense of self and use the mundane world as fodder for the evolution and healing of our soul.

The short stories, scientific facts, ancient wisdom and New Age thinking presented in Quest gives us paradigms, tools, and an applicable foundation to live an enlightened life in the mundane world.

The Two Questions that will set you free

In order to stay true to our Great Quest, I present two questions that will speed you on your way.

These questions are profound. Do not underestimate the value of these two questions because they are simple. These questions will challenge the very nature of who you are and how you chose to live this life.

Use them wisely, use them frequently.

Question one:

Who is it that I get to be?

Transformation maybe challenging, but it is not complicated.

Transformation occurs in the space between who we are and who we get to be. The mundane world gives us ample opportunities to step into our greatest potential: A courageous, embodied, enlightened, heart centered human being.

This is who I *get* to be.

Practice

This is a short contemplative exercise.

Bring yourself present. Tune into any body tension and let it relax. From this contemplative place, say each statement to yourself:

- This is who I *want* to be.
- This is who I *should* be.
- This is who I *get* to be.

Each statement holds a slightly different connotation.

Say them again.

- This is who I *want* to be.
- This is who I *should* be.
- This is who I *get* to be.

"This is who I *get* to be" is empowering.

It's much more empowering than, "This is who I *want* to be." Who I *want* to be takes us from the present and puts us into the future. Someday we will be that person…someday.

And it's more empowering than, "This is who I *should* be." *Should* is a guilt-laced position filled with the voices of what others think.

This is who I *get* to be. Simple. Powerful. Enlightening.

That's the query that keeps us on the path and aligns us with our Great Quest.

This is who I *get* to be when life is challenging - in times of conflict, discord, grief, and loss.

This is who I *get* to be when life is in sync- in times of love, kindness, generosity, patience and forgiveness.

This is who I *get* to be.

Question two:

What do I get to practice?

The answer is: you get to practice that which is not of habit.

That, in its simplicity, will allow you to live an enlightened, soulful, courageous life in the mundane world.

Practice:

This is also a contemplative exercise.

As a prompt: recall the paradigms, insights, inquiry, and practices from the previous chapters and your journal.

Have your journal and pen handy. Bring yourself to the present with a few deep abdominal breaths. Relax your shoulders. Listen to the sounds around you. Let your mind take a pause.

Think of a challenging situation that you currently face.

Consider that the universe has placed this challenge (and all other challenges) before you, as the most mundane of experiences, for one purpose: to become more enlightened.

Now, in your journal, respond to the following prompts:

The challenging situation: _____

This is how it makes me feel: _____

This is my initial, habitual, or limiting reaction to this challenge: ___
_____.

In this challenging situation, with how it makes you feel and even with your habitual reactions, complete this thought:

This is who I *get* to be, this is my great calling, this is my Great Quest: _____

This is what I *get* to practice: _____

Remember: you're not responding to the question of what you *want* to be or *should* be. This, like every mundane challenge, offers you the opportunity to **practice who you *get* to be.**

This is what I get to practice in times of hurt, angst, conflict, or grief.

As I *get to practice* - love, kindness, generosity, patience and forgiveness, this is who I become.

I become a courageous, embodied, enlightened, heart centered human being.

A Prayer to send you on your way

Thank you.

Thank you for helping me be who I get to be.

Thank you for offering me the opportunity to practice.

Use this frequently, use it wisely.

I stood there on the side of the road, watching people zip by. Wondering about their lives as I imagined they wondered about mine.

Moments later, a white '64 Chevy II pulled over. I shrugged my shoulders as if to shake off the stable middle-class life I'd always known. I glanced into the car, then down the road, then back into the car.

I shrugged once more and hopped in.

SELECTED BIBLIOGRAPHY

Barlett, Richard. *The Physics of Miracles.* Hillsboro OR. Beyond Words, 2009

Brennan, Barbara. *Hands of Light.* New York. Bantam Books, 1988

Brennan, Barbara. *Light Emerging.* New York. Bantam Books, 1993

Brown, Brene'. *Daring Greatly.* New York. Gotham Books, 2012

Bruyere, Rosalyn. *Wheels of Light.* New York. Simon & Schuster, 1994

Chopra, Deepak. *Quantum Healing.* New York. Bantam Books, 1989

Eden, Donna. *Energy Medicine for Women.* New York. Penguin Group, 2008

Forrest, Steven. *The Inner Sky.* San Diego CA. ACS Publications, 1997

Katie, Byron. *Loving What Is.* New York. Harmony Books, 2002

Kravits, Judith. *Breathe Deep, Laugh Loudly.* Center Sandwich New Hampshire. Free Breath Press, 2002

Lipton, Bruce. *The Biology of Belief.* Santa, Rosa CA. Mountain of Love/Elite Books, 2005

Monroe Institute Monroeinstitute.org

Myss, Caroline. *Defy Gravity*. New York. Hay House, 2009

Newton, Michael. *Journey of Souls*. Woodbury, MN. Llewellyn Publications, 2012

The Upledger Institute International Upledger.com

Yalom, Irvin. *The Theory and Practice of Group Psychotherapy*. New York. Basic Books, 1995

BIO

Dr. Steve Stroud has been a physician and teacher of Integrative Medicine, Traditional Chinese Medicine, Energy Medicine and trans-personal psychology for over 30 years. Dr. Stroud holds a Doctorate in Naturopathic Medicine and a Masters of Acupuncture. He has advanced training in Craniosacral therapy, Transformational Breath, and Matrix Energetics. For 11 years he was a core faculty member of the Barbara Brennan School of Healing. He is the founder and Executive Director of The Ripple Foundation, a nonprofit organization dedicated to the soulful and courageous adventure of transforming ourselves, our relationships, our community and the world. www.TheRippleFoundation.org

CPSIA information can be obtained
at www.ICGtesting.com
Printed in the USA
LVHW060757030623
748813LV00037B/852